The Famous Tales of Tenali Rama

Om Books International

First Published in 2024

Om Books International

Corporate & Editorial Office
A-12, Sector 64, Noida 201 301
Uttar Pradesh, India
Phone: +91 120 477 4100
Email: editorial@ombooks.com
Website: www.ombooksinternational.com

Sales Office
107, Ansari Road, Darya Ganj
New Delhi 110 002, India
Phone: +91 11 4000 9000
Email: sales@ombooks.com
Website: www.ombooks.com

ISBN: 978-81-96043-63-6

Printed in India

10 9 8 7 6 5 4 3 2 1

Contents

Tenali Meets King Rayalu

Tenali Rama was born in a village called Tenali, in the kingdom of Vijaynagar, ruled by King Sri Krishna Deva Rayalu. Tenali, his original name being Ramakrishnan, had taken his name from the village where he came from.

Tenali wanted to be a part of King Rayalu's court and very soon, he made way to the royal palace.

Tenali reached the palace, and went in unannounced, interrupting a dance performance that was going on in the court. This enraged King Rayalu and he ordered his guards to capture Tenali immediately. He was to be to be beheaded the next day. Tenali's mind, which always worked very fast, had already decided on a way to escape this punishment.

As the guards arrived in prison to take Tenali away, he first demanded that being a brahmin he needed to recite his prayers before his execution. The soldiers had to fulfil his last wish. So Tenali recited his prayers first and then ate to his heart's delight.

Tenali was now ready to meet his end, but insisted that he should be killed while in the river. That way he could chant Lord Rama's name and then flow away with the river. The guards agreeing to this request, took Tenali to the river that flowed through the city. Tenali went into the water, and stood there with only his head peeping out of the water. As the guard tried to swipe his sword across his head, Tenali would dip his head into the water. This made the guard miss Tenali's head — each and every time he tried!

The guards gave up finally, and took Tenali back to the king, explaining all that had happened. Though the king was pleased to hear about Tenali's quick-wit, he decided to give him another chance to prove his intelligence. This time the king insisted that Tenali's execution take place by elephants.

So the guards took Tenali to the edge of the nearby forest and put him inside a hole that they had dug in the ground for him. As they went back to fetch the elephants, Tenali started thinking of a way to get out of the hole and save his life.

Just then, a hunchback washerman, carrying a load of clothes on his back, passed by the hole. On seeing Tenali, he enquired as to why he was sitting in a hole. Tenali replied, that he too was a washerman and had developed a hunchback, carrying load on his back. On his doctor's advice, he was sitting in the mud hole.

Tenali further declared that his back was completely cured now! The washerman too, wanted to try the same remedy. So Tenali got himself pulled out of the hole and helped the washerman get into it. As the washerman's clothes had to be delivered to the palace, Tenali offered to do the job for him.

The washerman realised that he had been tricked when he saw the guards arrive with the elephants.

King Rayalu now was very pleased with Tenali and invited him to join his court.

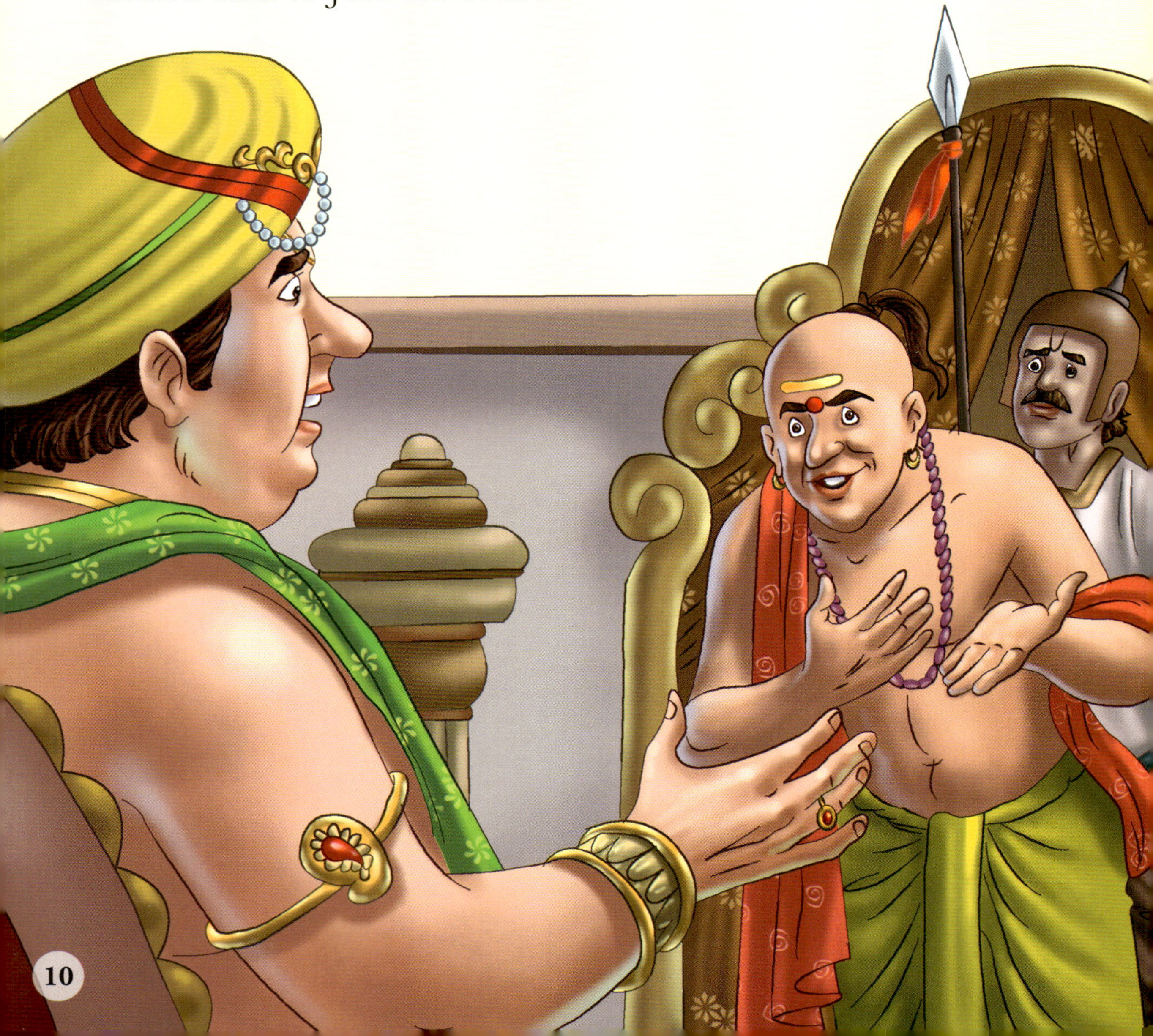

The Last Wish

There was great sorrow in the kingdom of Vijaynagar this one time. King Sri Krishna Deva Rayalu's mother had taken seriously ill. And the royal physicians had informed the king that due to her old age, there was nothing much that they could do for her anymore. This made the king very sad.

One morning, the royal mother called for her son. When King Rayalu arrived, she said, “My son, I know that I shall die very soon. But before I go, can you grant me my one last wish?”

Close to tears, King Rayalu replied, “Yes mother, please tell what it is that you want, and I shall do it for you.”

“I want to eat a mango for the last time, my son. Do you think you can get me one, before my soul leaves my body?”

Though it was early summer, Rayalu’s soldiers still found a basketful of mangoes for his mother. But the old lady died before they could give her the basket.

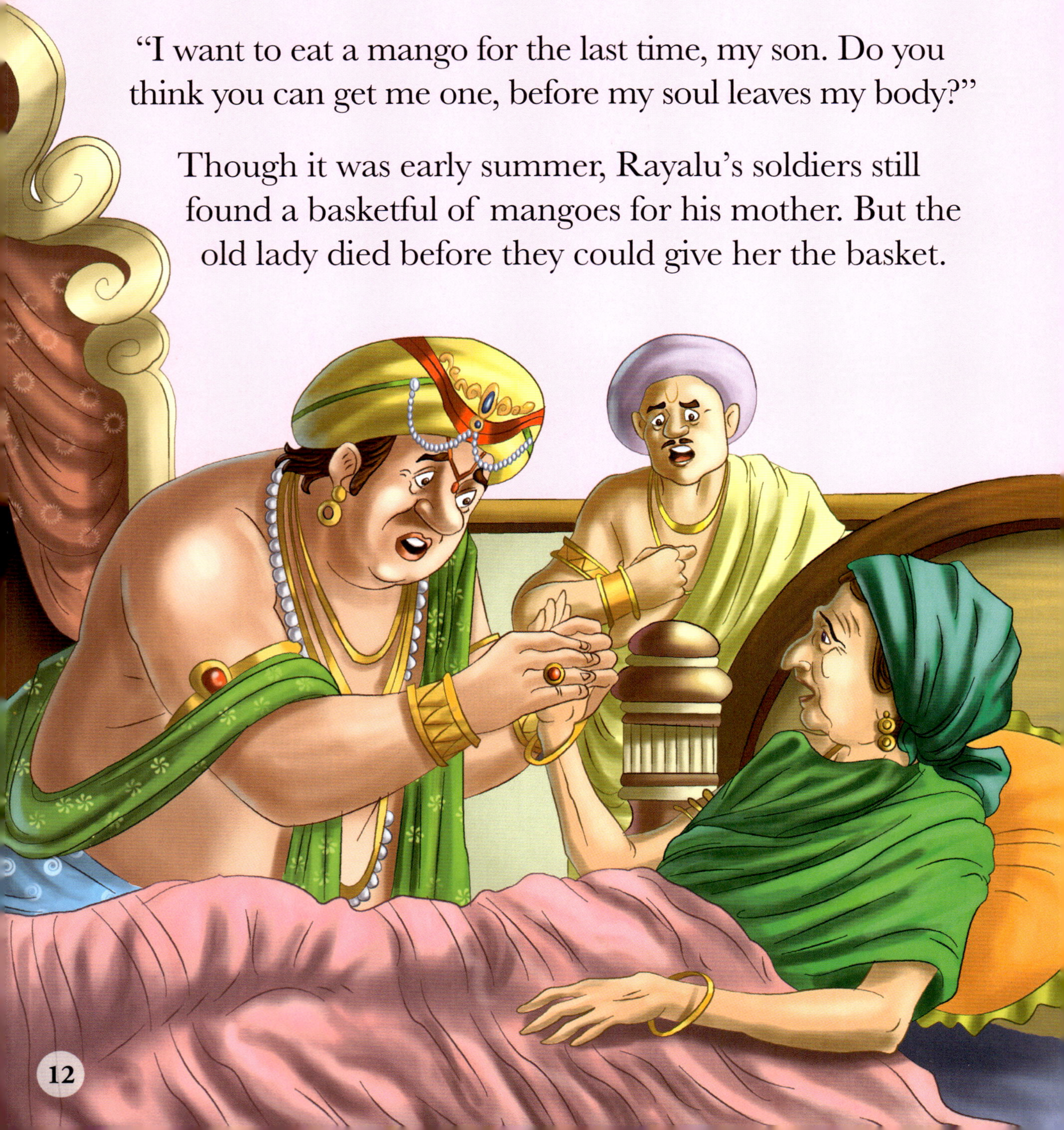

King Rayalu was extremely upset on his mother's death. He felt even worse, because he could not grant her last wish.

One day, he went to Thathacharya, the royal priest of the court of Vijaynagar and sought his advice on the matter. Thathacharya pondered over the issue for a while, and declared, "O King! As I see it, there is perhaps one way out. Your mother loved to give alms to the poor. Maybe you should get some mangoes made of gold and distribute them amongst brahmins. That should make her happy!"

Word soon spread through the empire like wildfire that the king was giving away golden mangoes to brahmins. Long queues started forming outside the palace, as people came from all over for the mangoes.

Consequently, the gold reserves of the state were also falling and though Chief Minister Thimmarusu pleaded with the king to stop, all his efforts fell on deaf ears. Not knowing what to do, Thimmarusu decided to tell Tenali Rama about it.

After hearing the whole matter, Tenali said, "Alright! I have understood what the problem is. Please go back to the court and leave the matter to me."

Next day, Tenali asked the guards to first send the brahmins to him. As all the brahmins gathered before him, Tenali said, "My friends, there has been a slight change in the whole donation process. The king will now hand over the golden mangoes only to those people who bear a blister from him. I will first burn your backs and only then can you stand in line for your golden mango. Is that clear?"

The prospect of the golden mango was more tempting than the blister. Therefore, all brahmins allowed Tenali to burn their backs. This went on till late afternoon, till a brahmin came up to Tenali and requested, "Can I get two mangoes if you burn my back twice?" Tenali was more than happy to oblige.

As the king gave him only one mango, the distraught brahmin said, "My lord, look… I have two burns on my back. Please give me another mango." The king was dumbfounded at what the brahmin had to say. He soon got the whole picture from the brahmin.

"What is this Tenali? Why have you been torturing these poor people? Have you gone mad?" he demanded.

Tenali Rama simply replied, "My lord, I was just following your methods to give my dead mother's soul eternal peace. You see, when my mother died recently, she kept wishing to cauterize her back so that she could remain young. But I never bothered to do anything about it and she died. I thought that by following your principle, maybe my mother too would finally find peace. Was I wrong in thinking that way, My Lord?"

King Rayalu understood that Tenali was trying to teach him a lesson. He even remembered Thimmarusu's warnings about the depleting gold reserves. Having learnt his lesson, Rayalu immediately called off the whole golden mango donation exercise and thanked Tenali and Thimmarusu for their loyalty.

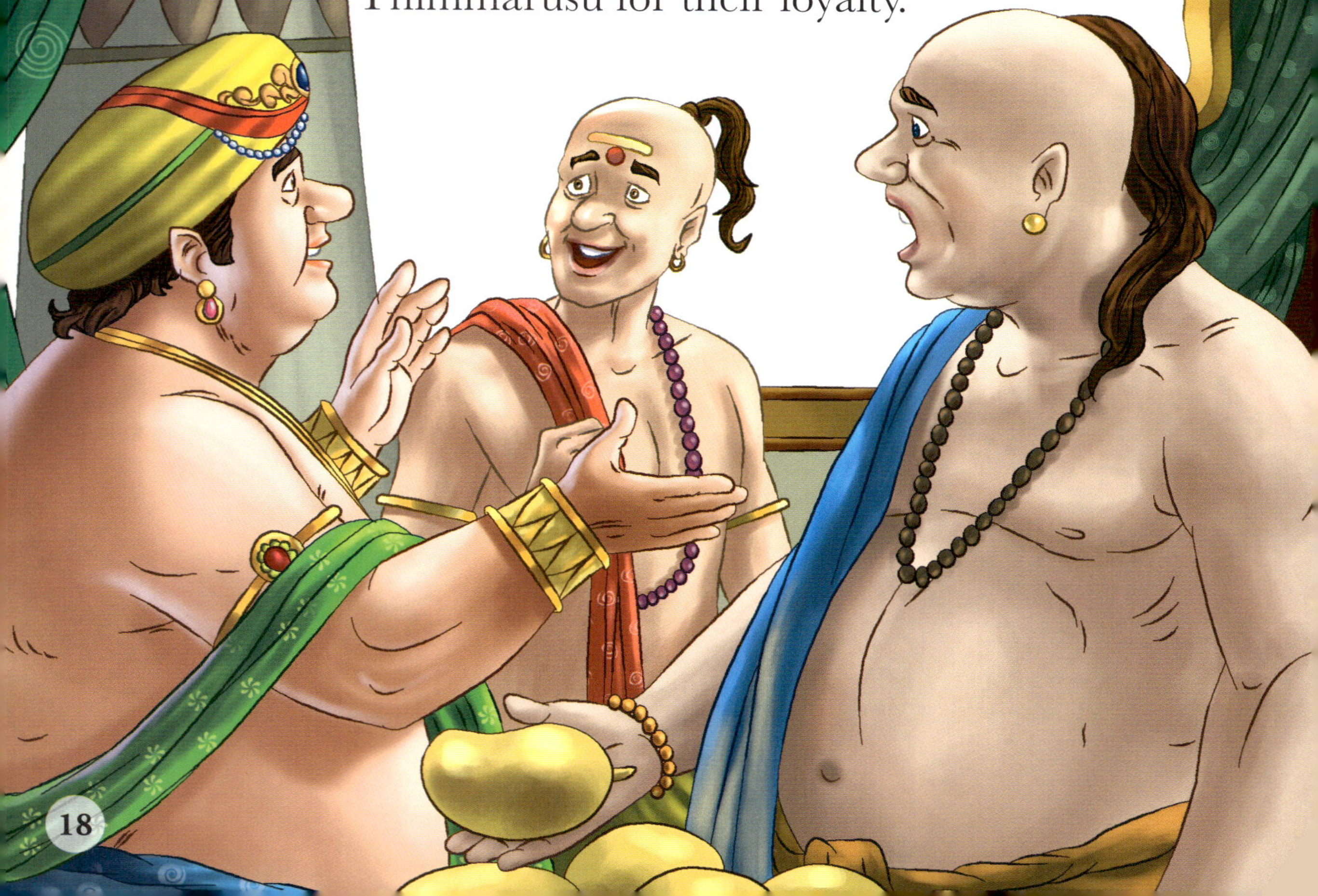

The Visit to Delhi

Once upon a time, there was a great war between the forces of Adil Shah from the northern part of India and the army of King Sri Krishna Deva Rayalu. As the war continued without any side being able to gain control over the other, both kingdoms decided to end the war.

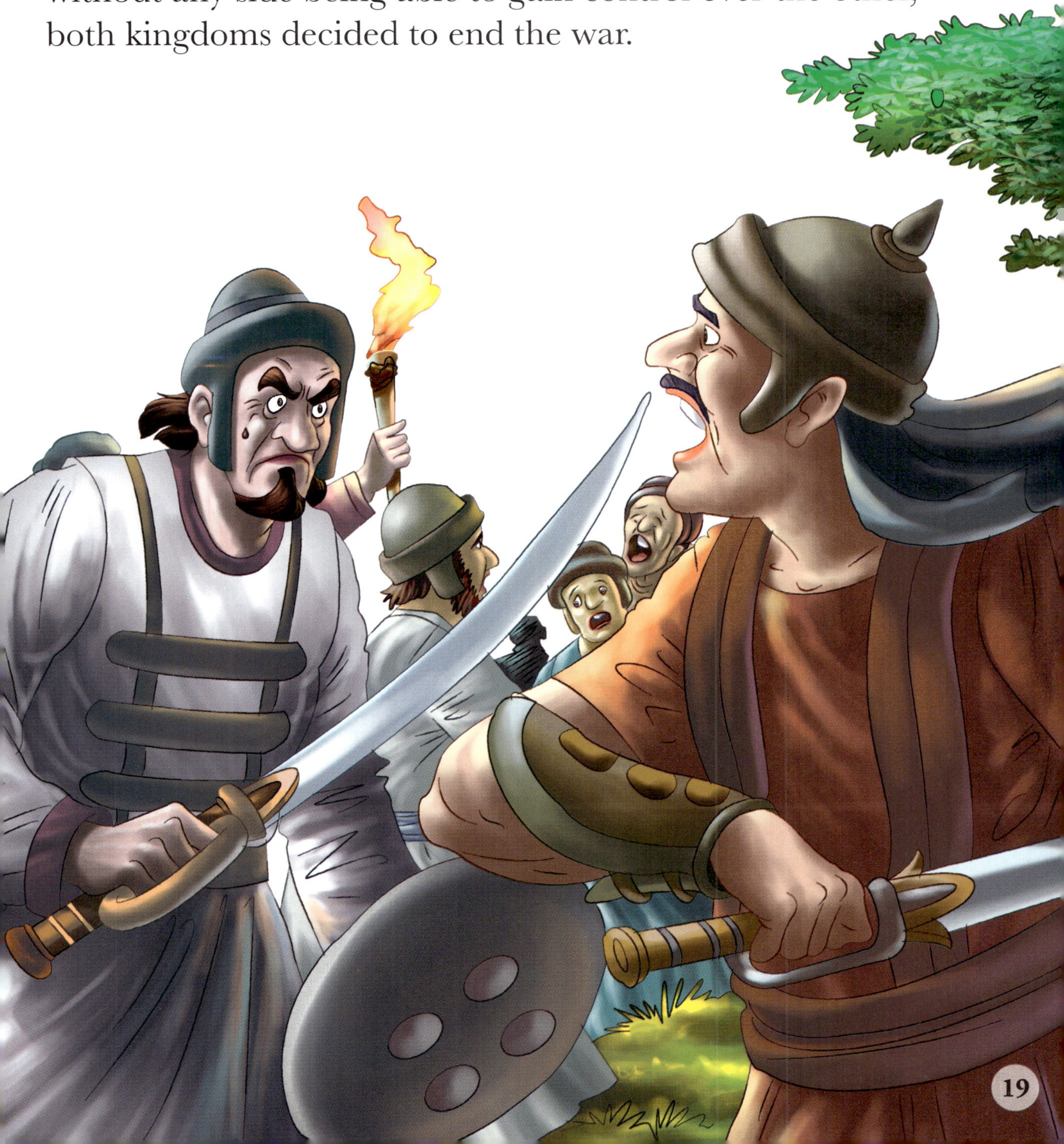

When King Rayalu, with a huge band of court poets and philosophers, reached Delhi, they were given a red carpet welcome and were treated very cordially. As the day progressed, Adil Shah requested the scholars and poets of Vijaynagar to recite passages from the Mahabharata.

As the poets recited more and more verses from the great epic, Adil Shah was so swayed by it that he asked Rayalu to ask his scholars to rewrite the Mahabharata, wherein they would talk about Adil Shah and his friends as the Pandavas and their enemies as Kauravas. This shocked all the visitors.

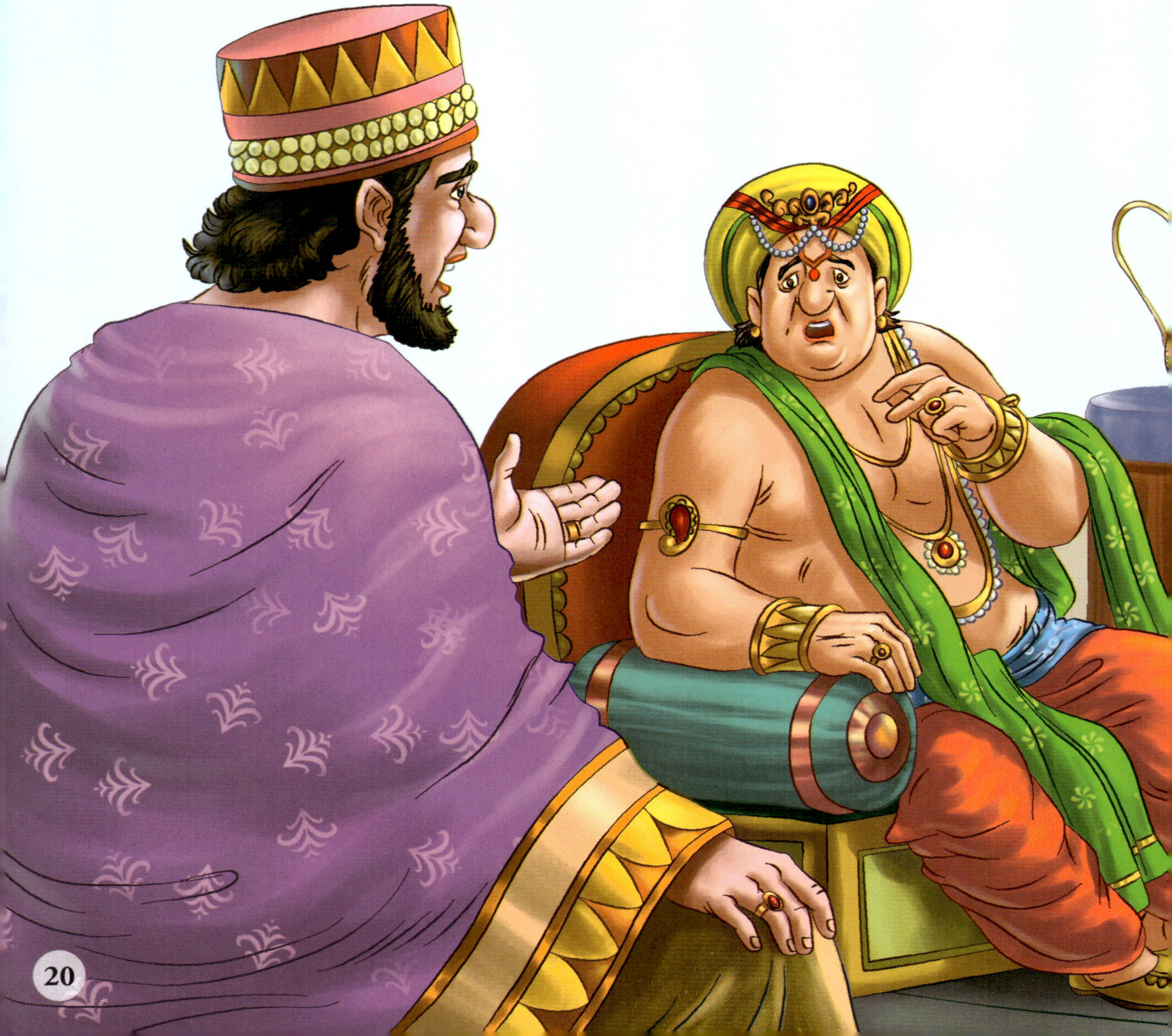

As they pondered over the situation they were in, Tenali Rama came up to King Rayalu and suggested, "I have the solution to the problem, Your Majesty. Please leave the matter to me."

Though the king and all the other scholars were not sure as to what Tenali's solution might be, they decided to let him tackle the issue.

Next morning, as the court resumed, Adil Shah spoke once again about the Mahabharata. Tenali immediately walked up to him and said, “Your Majesty, we shall definitely consider your wish – but before that, we think there is something that you should know. If you could grant me a few moments in private with you, there is something that I need to tell you.”

Hearing about Tenali Rama's proposal, Adil Shah finally granted his request. Once they were alone, Tenali began, "My Lord, we have started writing the Mahabharata with you as Yudhisthira, and your friends as the other Pandavas. However, we have stumbled upon a block. You see, all five Pandava brothers were married to Draupadi. So in that regard…"

Even before he could complete his sentence, Adil Shah roared, “What? I demand that you stop writing Mahabharata or any other such book. This cannot be accepted.”

“But Sire, we have already begun work as per your request…” protested Tenali.

“If you want a lifetime of peace between our two kingdoms, then you will stop immediately!” So saying Adil Shah walked off, leaving Tenali Rama smiling within.

Handful of Grain

There was once, in a town called Simhapuri in the kingdom of Vijaynagar, a beautiful but proud woman called Vidyullatha. She was an extremely educated and talented woman and would always boast about her wisdom.

One day, she put a board outside her house, which said 'One thousand gold coins as reward to the person who can impress the lady of the house. Competitors will be judged on their wit, humour and wisdom'.

On seeing this offer, many scholars decided to try their luck in dazzling Vidyullatha and winning the reward. However, they all came out of her house, hanging their heads in shame.

One morning, as the competitors began queuing up outside the lady's house, a man selling firewood kept screaming outside, "Premium firewood, premium firewood! Burns better, burns longer!"

Unable to concentrate on her contest, Vidyullatha decided to go and buy all the firewood this man was selling, so that he would leave. But as she made the man her offer of purchase, he turned around and said, "I am sorry lady, but all this firewood will cost you a handful grain. Can you give me that?"

Vidyullatha was amazed at the price this man was asking. She impatiently said, "Come along! Drop all that here and come with me. I shall give you much more grain."

The vendor was also adamant. He unloaded all the logs he was carrying on his head and yelled, "Please be clear lady. I will not bargain with you. A handful grain is all that I want. Please make the payment. I will not accept anything else."

His curt replies infuriated Vidyullatha. She snapped back, "Just do as you are told. I said I will give you your grain, so just come with me."

"If you cannot pay me the handful grain, you will have to pay me a thousand gold coins and also remove this board from here," the vendor chirped.

The argument went on with both parties screaming at each other. Vidyullatha could not understand what the vendor's problem was. Finally, it was decided that this matter should be taken to the court of justice.

Vidyullatha told the judge, "Your Honour, I do not know what is wrong with this man. He said that he wanted a handful of grain for his logs and I said that I shall give him more. But then he said that if I do not give him his handful grain, he would charge me a thousand gold coins for them. I think he is crazy!"

As the judge turned to the vendor, he replied in his defence, "My Lord, the woman is telling the truth. I asked her to pay me a handful grain for my logs. I think the point where she got confused was that she felt I was asking for a handful of grain. But no, I was asking for a handful grain. If she cannot pay the price that was settled at the beginning, she should pay me the thousand gold coins as a fine, shouldn't she?"

The judge admitted that the vendor was indeed right and awarded the case in his favour. However, he did not admit that the vendor was actually Tenali Rama, who on hearing about this woman's arrogance, had decided to teach her a lesson.

The Divine Clothes

One day, an extremely beautiful woman entered the court at Vijaynagar, where King Sri Krishna Deva Rayalu was busy dealing with the matters of the state. With her pleasing voice and gestures the woman was able to grab the attention of the king in no time. She then placed before him a small box, perhaps meant to hold her earrings, and took out a sari from it.

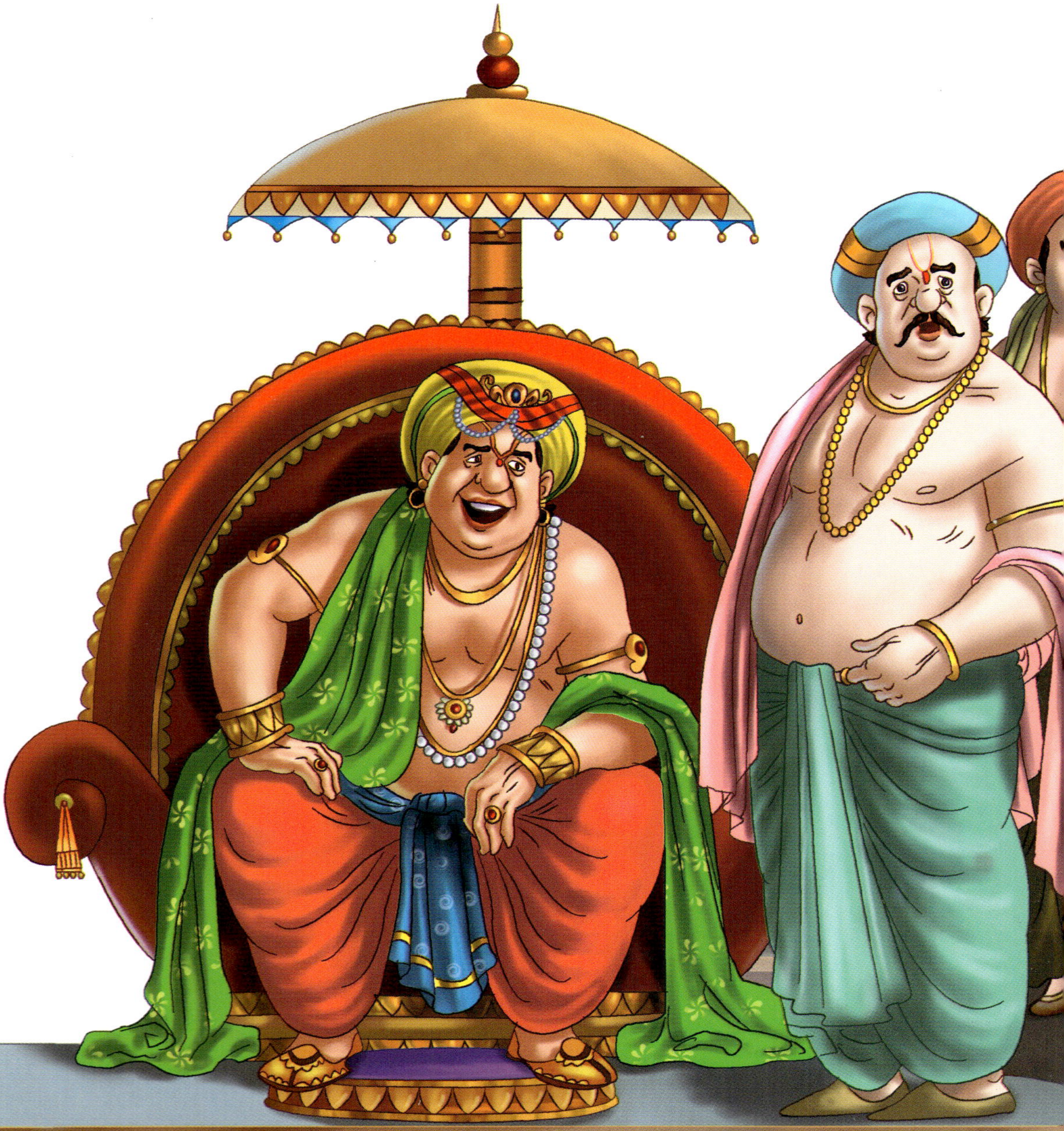

She placed the sari before King Rayalu and declared, "Oh great king of Vijaynagar, behold the work of some divine weavers. They are so gifted that they are the only ones who can weave a celestial fabric that is unseen to the human eye. With your support and patronage, we shall work towards producing such clothes for you."

Rayalu was extremely impressed with what he saw. He immediately asked the lady to come and live in the palace with her divine weavers. He even arranged for her to get a sum of money, wherein she would present before the king a sari made out of this celestial fabric in a year.

Very soon, the year ended and though the lady had been living in the palace and utilising the funds sanctioned by the king, her sari was not yet ready. Curious, the king asked his guards to pay her a visit in her chambers and find out what the problem was.

The guards, on arriving at the place where the weavers were working, saw them drag their fingers over air. They all appeared to be sewing, but they did not have any fabric to work on. On asking the beautiful lady this question, she replied, "Oh, but they are working on the divine fabric. If you or your parents have ever sinned, you will not be able to see the sari they have made. However, I am sure that you can clearly see what is in front of you, oh guard!"

Unable to say that he saw nothing, the guard lied. Soon it was time for the woman to present her creation before the king. Needless to say, she pointed to the air and asked the king to see the sari. Turning to Tenali Rama, the king whispered, "I cannot see anything Tenali… Am I the sinner, or do I bear the curse of my parents' sins?"

Tenali Rama had of course understood the woman's game by then. He thought about it for a moment and then turned to the woman and said,

"Oh lady, the king is indeed so enamoured by what you have presented before him, that he wishes you to wear it yourself and display its real beauty."

The lady realised that Tenali Rama had caught her. Without trying to find her way out of the mess, she jumped at the king's feet and begged for mercy. King Rayalu smiled at Tenali.

The Thieves

King Sri Krishna Deva Rayalu of Vijaynagar would often visit jails to check on the convicts. On one such visit, he was confronted by two thieves who begged him to reduce their punishment. They even went on to describe to the king how

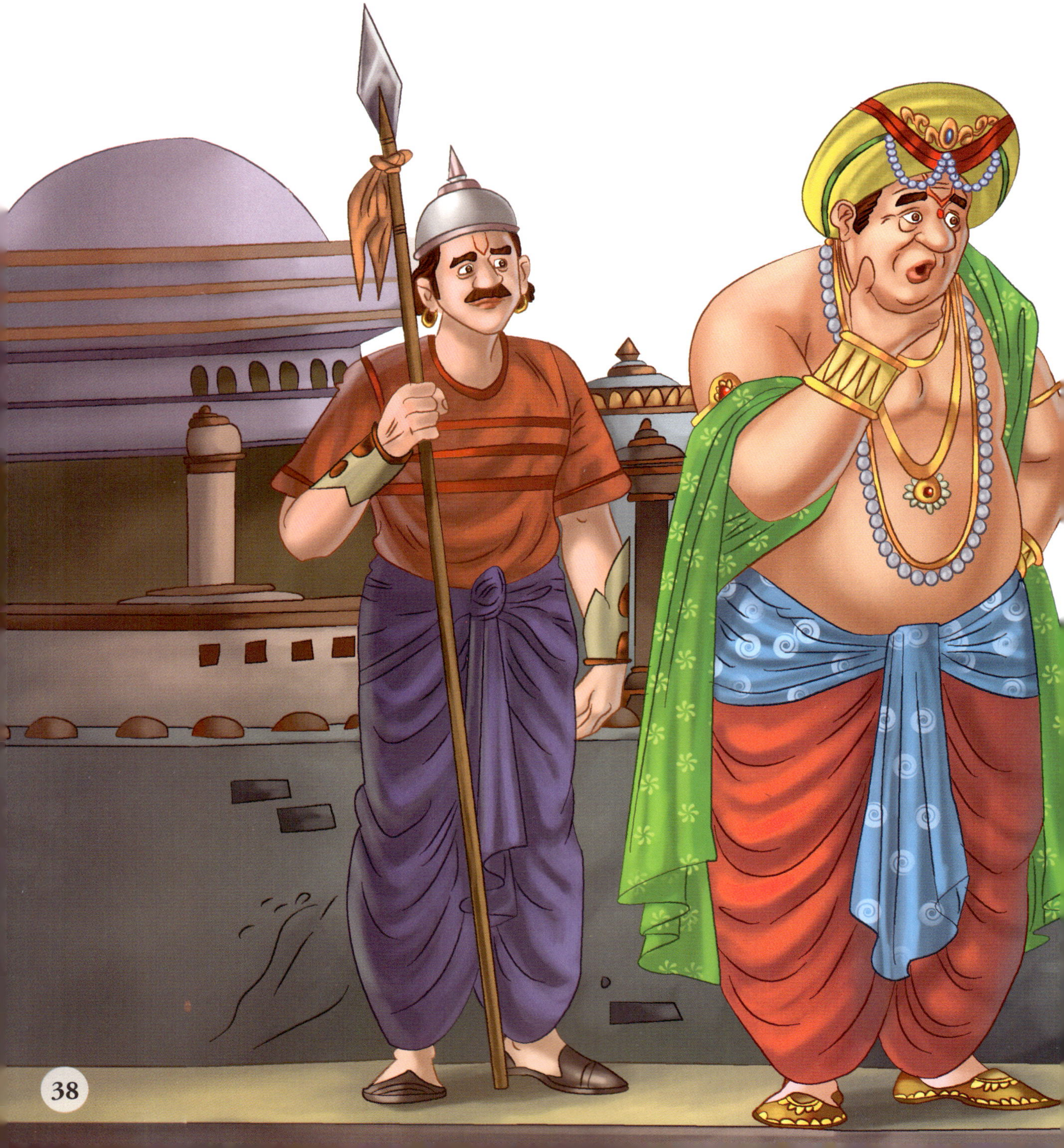

stealing was a Vedic art. Looking through their cunning, the king decided to catch them red-handed. He said, "Alright! Let me make a deal. You two thieves will have to steal from the house of my minister, Tenali Rama. If you do it without getting caught, you shall be freed from prison. However, there is only one condition – you cannot harm the household."

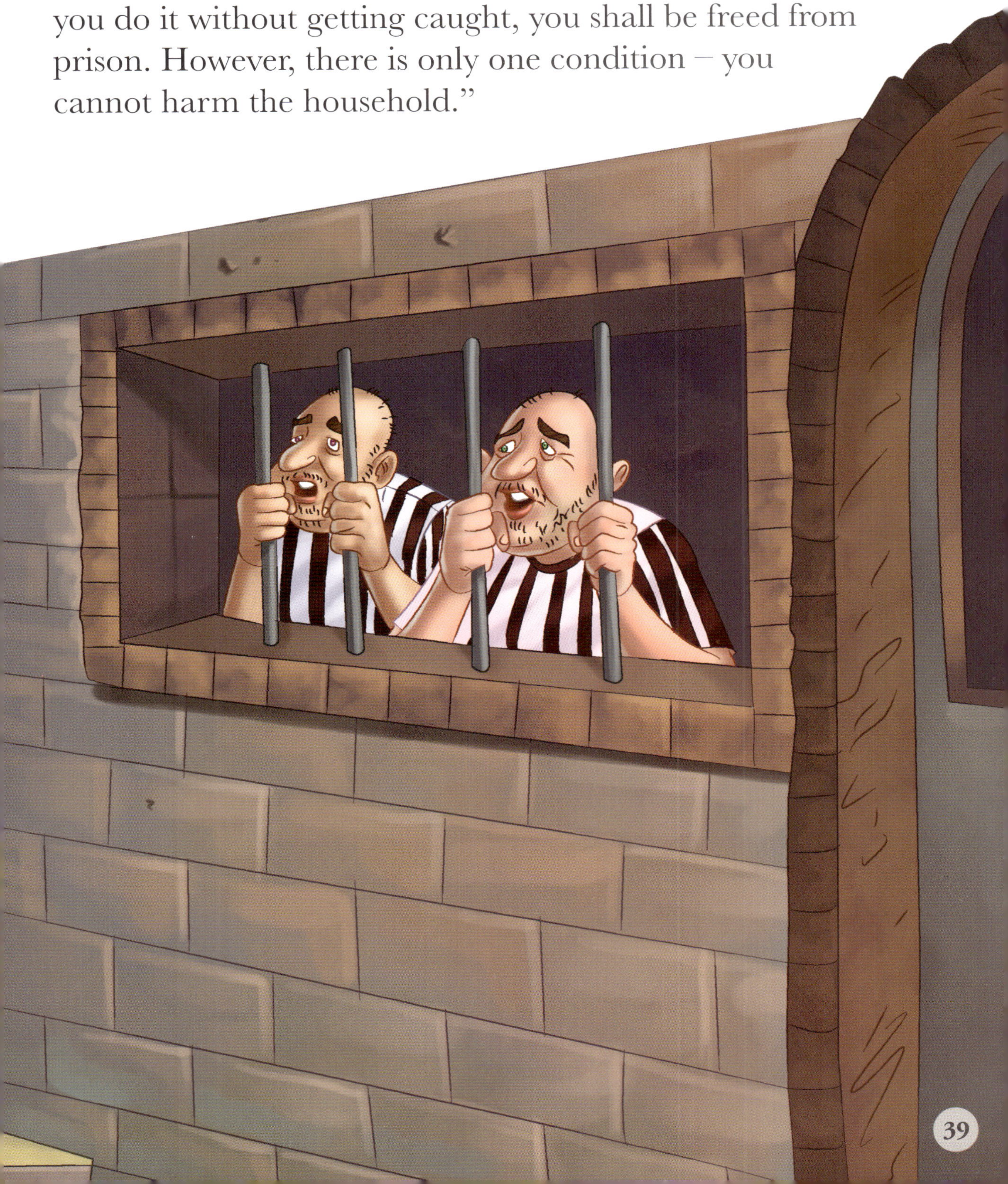

That night, the thieves were let out from prison, so that they could go and rob from Tenali Rama's house. Tenali at that time was busy tending to the garden he was growing around his house. Being an alert man, he at once noticed the two thieves hiding behind some bushes. He called out to his wife, "I hear that two burglars have escaped from prison. Please bring all the jewellery and valuables that we have in the house and keep them here so that they are safe."

Soon the burglars saw Tenali and his wife drag a heavy box to the well and throw it inside. They felt that this was indeed their lucky day as stealing from Tenali's house would not be any trouble at all. As soon as Tenali went back inside, they walked over to the well. One of them stood guard and the other one went down to retrieve the box.

As there was a lot of water in the well, he called out to the other thief and asked him to help him pull some water out of the well. As they kept dumping the water on to the garden, Tenali walked back quietly behind them and started directing the water towards the plants.

The thieves went on pouring water over the courtyard for quite some time. Once the water level in the well was reduced, they went back in to bring out the box. As they managed to come out of the well, they were shocked to see that the box only contained stones. Suddenly they heard Tenali speak from behind, "Come on boys… only two more plants need to be watered. It's almost dawn. Let's finish the job fast."

Realising that Tenali had outsmarted them completely, the two thieves ran back straight to prison. King Rayalu met them the next day in prison and said, "Well, it looks like you'll still need to master the Vedic art of stealing. You can do that during your stay here for the rest of the term. The day you can rob from Tenali Rama, you will know that you are the true masters."

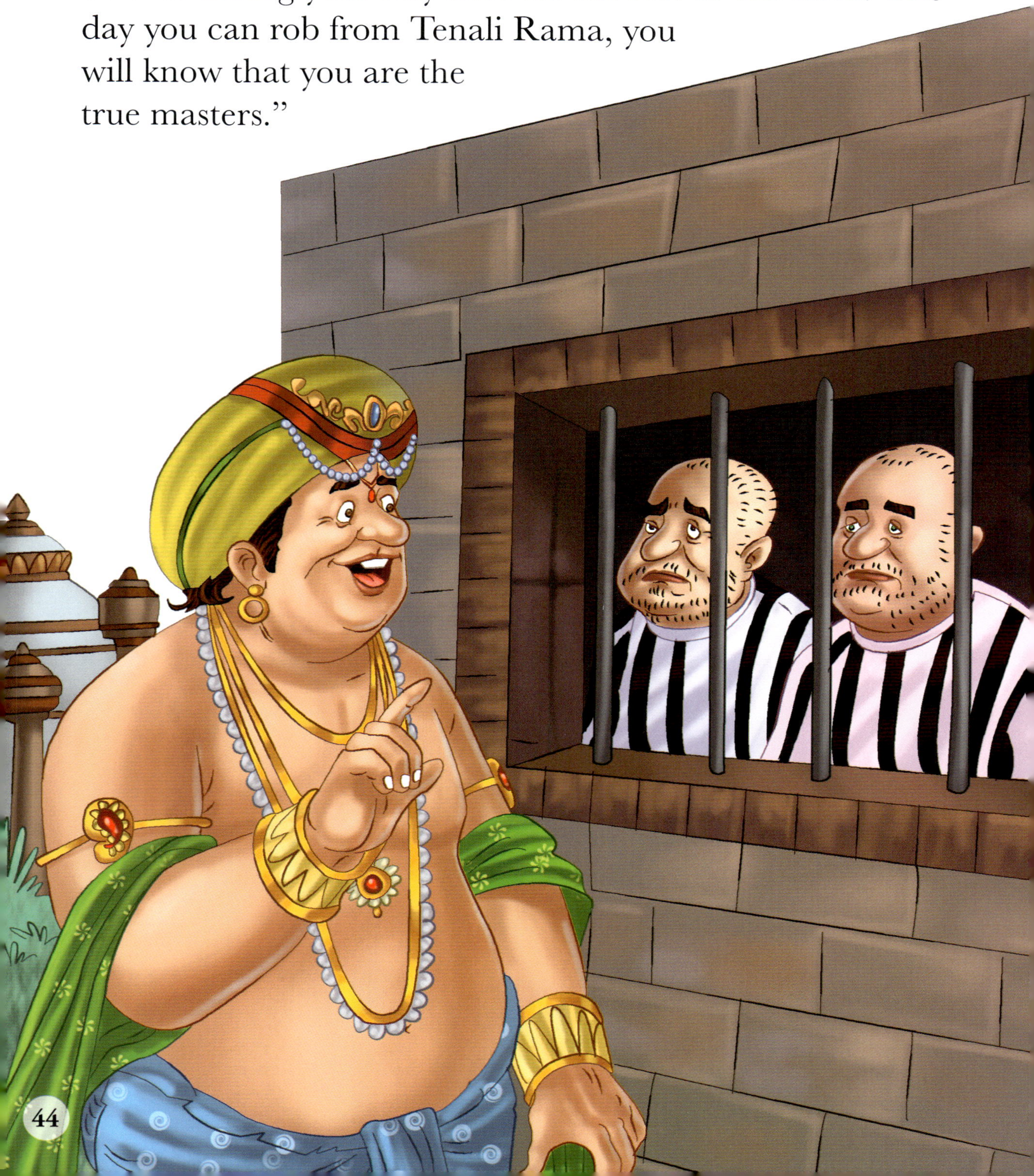

The Marriage of the Wells

The Sultans who ruled Delhi were always on the lookout for some issue which they could raise with the kings of the neighbouring states, so that they could declare war on them and then rule their kingdoms. One day, the Sultan of Delhi hit upon an idea, which he felt would give him the opportunity to attack Vijaynagar, the kingdom ruled by Sri Krishna Deva Rayalu.

He sent over a messenger with an invitation for King Rayalu. The message said, “We cordially invite all the wells from the state of Vijaynagar to grace the occasion of marriage between two wells in Delhi. The participation of these wells in the marriage affairs is indeed compulsory and non-acceptance of the invitation will prove to be an insult to the Delhi Sultanate.” Beyond this, the message also contained the time and date of this so-called marriage between two wells.

King Rayalu and his ministers were completely dumbstruck at what they heard. Through their repeated questioning, the messenger said nothing and soon went back to where he came from. King Rayalu could understand that the Sultan was just looking for an opportunity to declare war on Vijaynagar. He could not find a way to escape from the situation. Even Chief Minister Thimmarusu was helpless in this matter. After some time, it was agreed that the matter would be entrusted to the court poet, Tenali Rama.

Tenali Rama took a good look at the invitation and burst out laughing. He turned to the courtiers and said, “Is that all? You couldn’t find a solution to this simple problem? Please leave everything to me. I’ll draft a suitable reply to the Sultan and you shall see that there is absolutely nothing to worry about.”

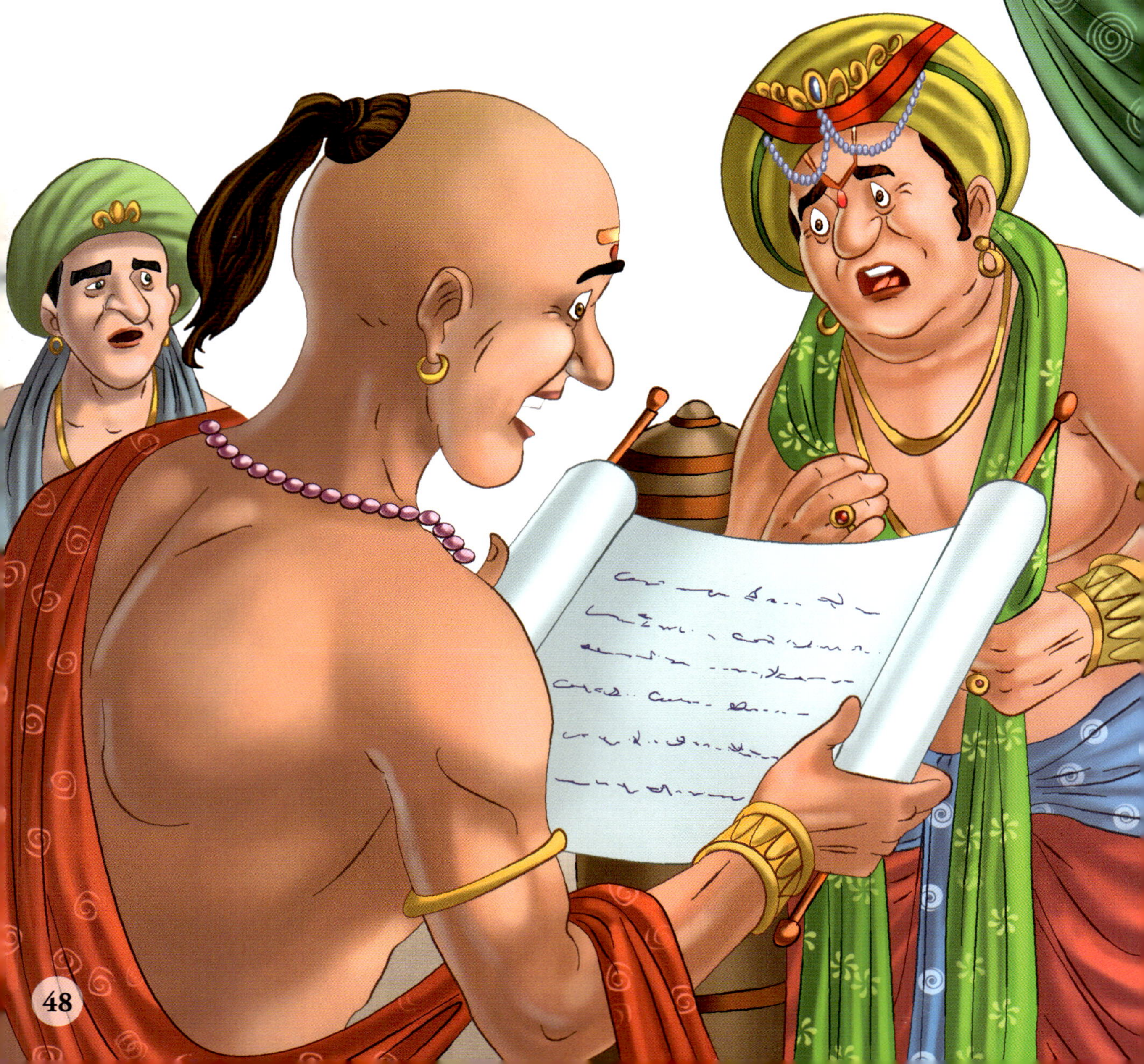

Next morning, the court had assembled as usual, but there was panic everywhere. Even the king was not certain as to what Tenali Rama had in store for them. Tenali walked up to the king and said, "Here you are my Lord. Please go through it once…"

The message read: “Oh illustrious Sultan of Delhi, it was indeed very kind of you to remember us and our wells on this occasion of great joy in your state. However, as regards our attendance at the wedding of your wells, our wells are still very offended that you did not send your wells to their weddings. I suggest that the only way to change their minds would be to send your wells to our kingdom, so that they can invite them to the wedding personally. After that I am sure

that we can all peacefully travel to your kingdom and take part in the celebrations."

When the Sultan heard the message in his court some days later, he was more amused than enraged. He marvelled at the brilliance of the Vijaynagar Empire and sent back a huge load of gifts for King Rayalu with his messenger.

A 'Satisfying' Ramayana Recital

Once upon a time, when the town of Vikram Simhapuri was under the rule of King Sri Krishna Deva Rayalu, there lived an extremely beautiful woman there, by the name of Kanchana Mala. Now this woman was known through the whole city as being extremely cunning. She would ask scholars to give her a satisfying recital of the Ramayana. If they succeeded in satisfying her, she would give them huge rewards. However, if they failed to do so, then they would be compelled to work in her house as her slaves. As more and more scholars took her offer, the number of slaves in her house kept increasing. None of the scholars were able to satisfy her.

One day, Tenali Rama visited the city Simhapuri on some official business of the king. As he sat down to discuss the city's problems with the scholars, he was informed about the scheming Kanchana Mala. An old scholar told him, "Everyone went to her to claim the reward, but the woman could never be satisfied. Many great minds are now working

in her house as her slaves." Tenali Rama was shocked to hear this. He decided to teach this woman a lesson. He told the scholars, "Will one of you please go and tell her that I will be calling upon her in the evening to recite the Ramayana. I guarantee that she will be extremely satisfied with what I have to offer."

Knowing that Kanchana Mala's time was up, the scholars decided to go and give her the message. By evening, Tenali Rama visited Kanchana Mala. She greeted him with warmth and welcomed him into her house. Tenali said, "Madam, I vouch that when I recite the Ramayana, you will feel that it is happening before your very eyes. You shall indeed be satisfied this time."

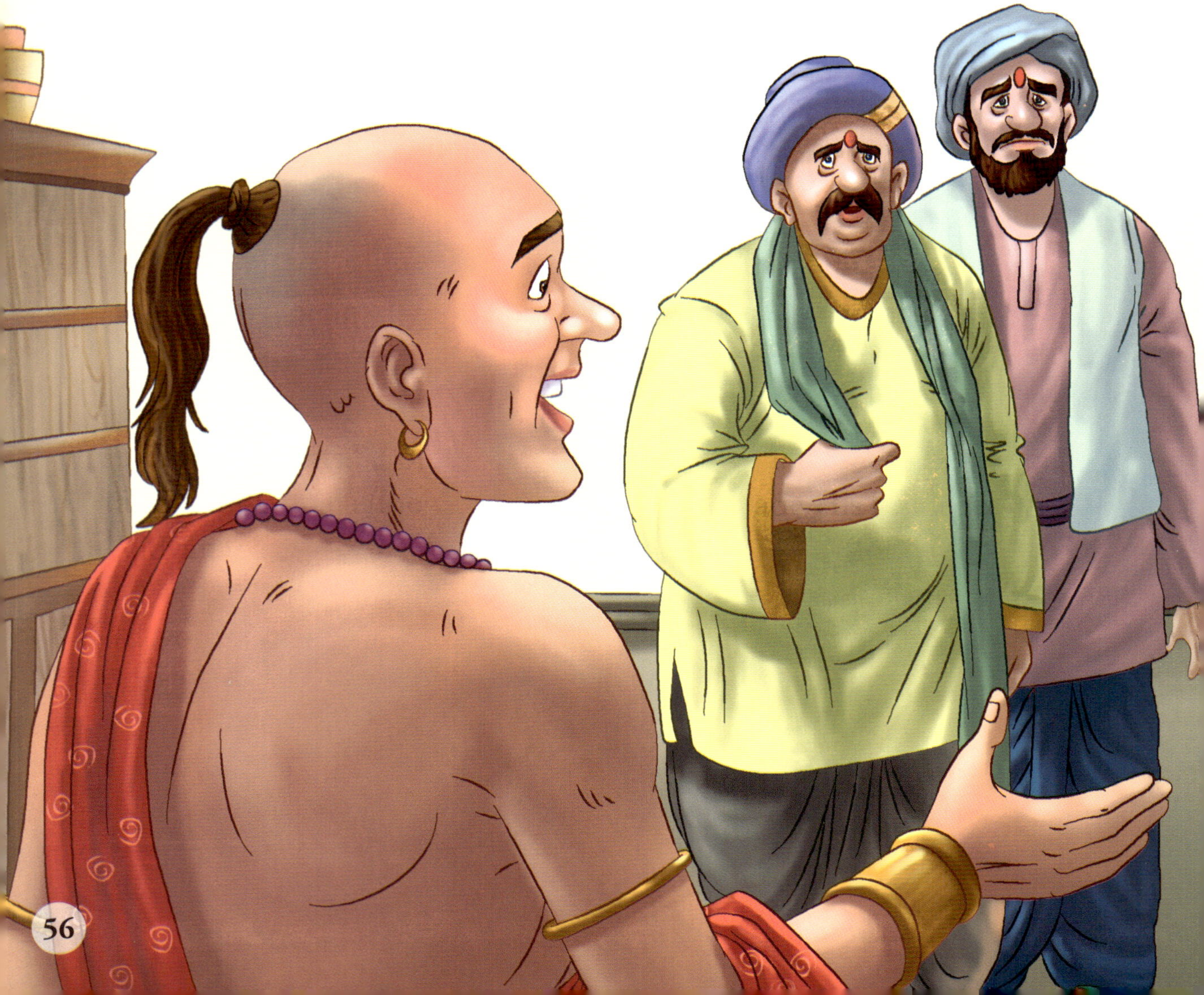

Kanchana Mala smiled and replied, "I am indeed looking forward to your recital Sir. However, I hope that you know about the reward and the punishment that may be in store for you later?"

"Yes, I am aware of all that. I, however, must ask you for one favour. You are not to stop me from carrying out my recital in anyway. I hope I have the liberty to do whatever I feel is necessary to satisfy you."

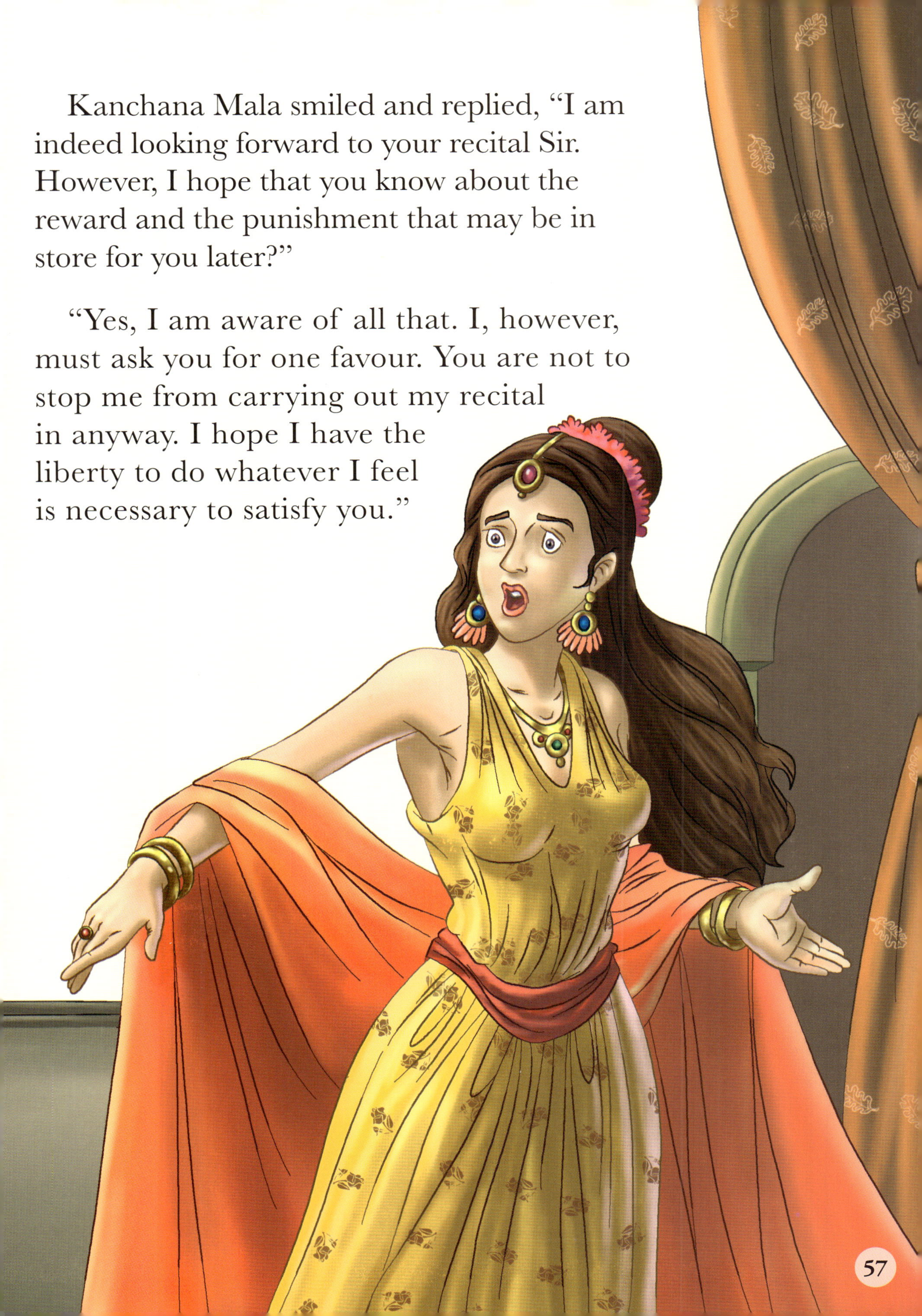

After Kanchana Mala's approval, Tenali started reciting the epic. After a point, he started jumping on her beds and spoke of the way in which Hanuman wrecked the city of Lanka. He broke most of the stuff that was there in the room and even set fire to her clothes. As she tried to protest, Tenali reminded her of the condition that he had set before he began his performance. Finally, in order to save herself, she ran out of the burning house and headed straight for the court of justice.

After hearing her story, the judge asked Tenali what he had to say in reply. Tenali Rama told him about how she had been cheating learned scholars and making them slaves in her house. The Judge understood Tenali's point and awarded the judgement in his favour. This also helped him in freeing the other scholars who were trapped in Kanchana Mala's house.

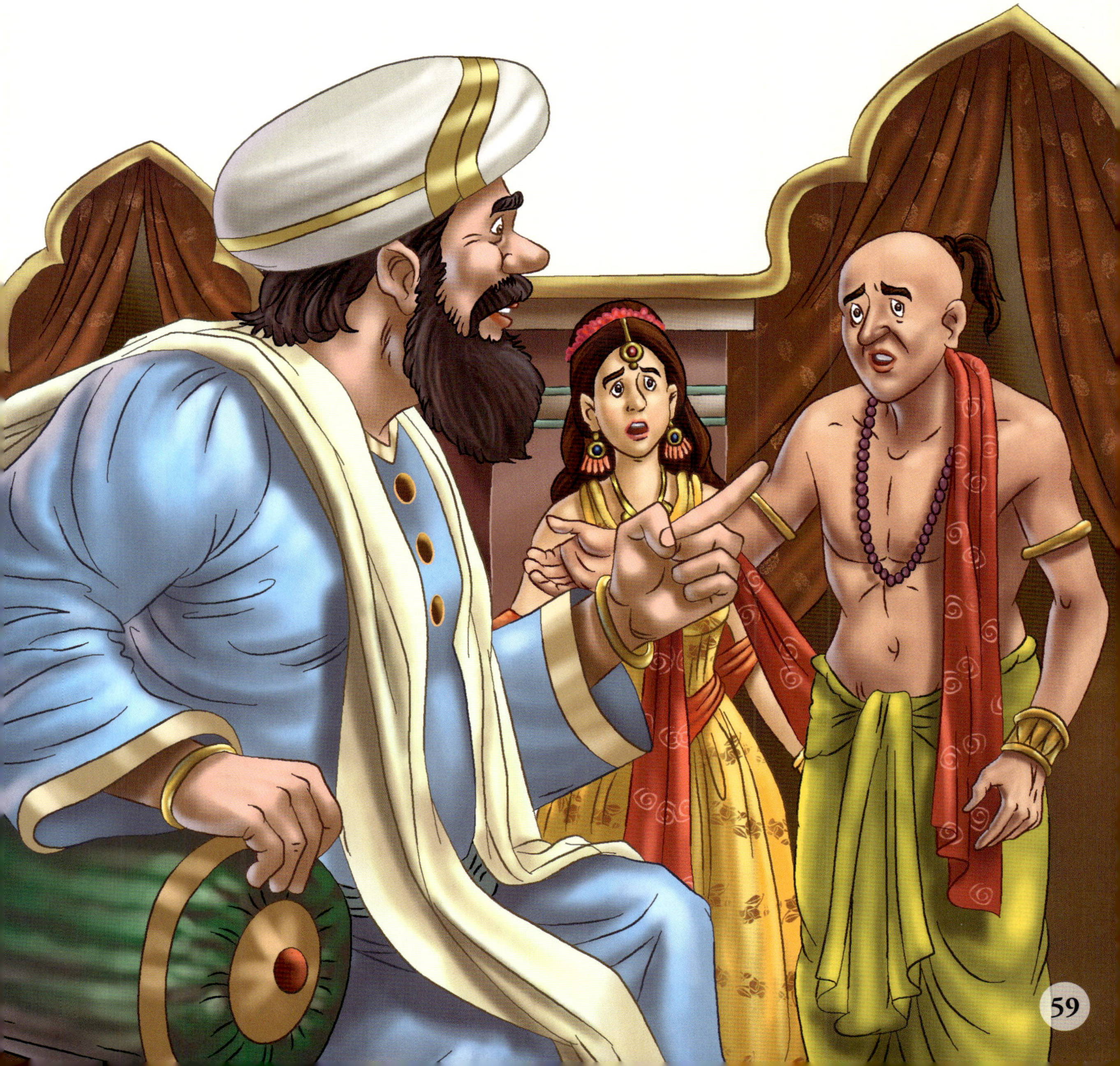

Black Dog White Cow

One morning, King Sri Krishna Deva Rayalu of the Vijaynagar Empire got up a little early from his sleep. Still sleepy, he ordered the guard standing there to fetch the barber. As he waited for the barber to arrive, King Rayalu once again fell back into deep sleep. When the barber saw the king asleep on his arrival, he was in a fix. Neither could he wake the king up, nor could he leave without carrying out his duties. Finally, after much deliberation, the barber decided to shave the king's beard and also cut his hair without disturbing his sleep.

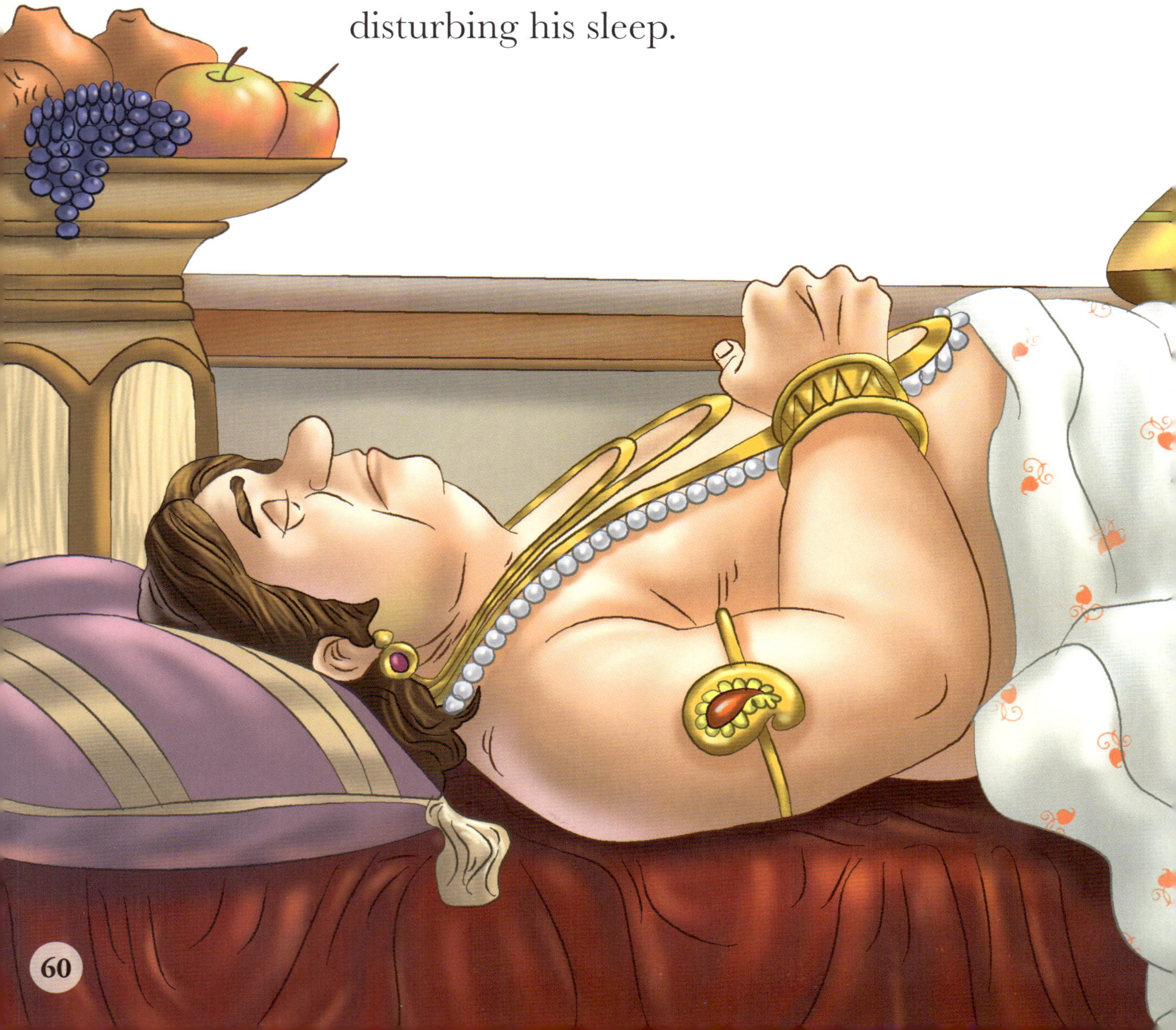

When King Rayalu woke up, he was enraged at not finding the barber there. As he got up to punish the barber, he saw his own reflection in the mirror and was amazed to see that he had already done his job. Very pleased with the barber, the king summoned him and said, "I am very impressed with what I see. I offer you a boon, so ask for anything that you desire."

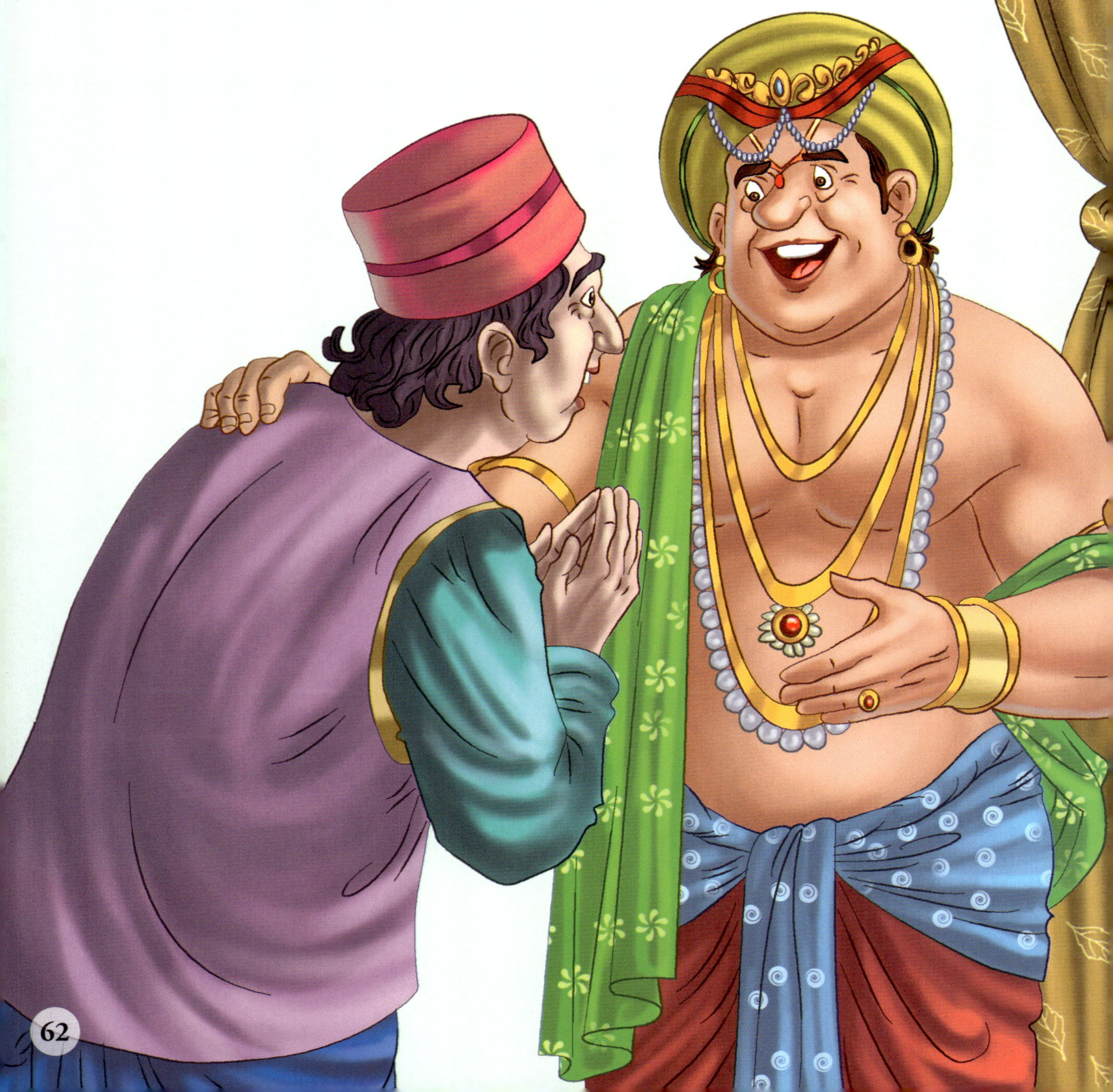

Overjoyed, the barber folded his hands and said, "My Lord, it has always been my fondest wish that I become a brahmin. Please make this wish of mine come true."

King Rayalu was surprised to hear the man's request, but told him that it would be done anyway. Next day, he called all the brahmins to court and told them about the barber's desire. "If you'll convert him into a brahmin, I shall give you big rewards." On hearing the word 'rewards', the brahmins immediately nodded and agreed to do the needful.

However, deep within their hearts they were extremely unhappy about the whole episode. They went to Tenali Rama and told him about it. "How can the king grant such a boon? How is this ever going to work?" Tenali asked them to return to their houses and get ready for the rituals the next day. Meanwhile, he would try and see if there was any way in which he could handle the situation.

Next morning, the king, the barber and the brahmins all gathered on the river bank where the puja had begun. Close by, Tenali Rama was also chanting some verses from the scriptures before a black dog, not paying any attention to the royal ceremony. Curious, the king walked up to him and asked him, "What is this that you are doing Tenali?"

"Oh, My Lord, I am actually transforming this black dog into a white cow..."

Taken aback, the king replied, "Tenali, have you gone mad? How can you change a black dog... or for that matter any dog into a cow?"

Tenali Rama humbly replied, “Why Sir, if that barber can be converted into a brahmin, why cannot I change a black dog into a white cow?”

Seeing through Tenali Rama’s argument, King Rayalu took back the boon and asked the brahmins to stop the ceremony.

The Death Penalty

Thathacharya was the Rajguru in the empire of Vijaynagar, where Sri Krishna Deva Rayalu ruled as the king.

Now Thathacharya was extremely jealous of Tenali Tenali. King Rayalu's court poet. In order to get at him, he would fill the king's ears with lies about Tenali; and enraged, the king would announce the death penalty for Tenali.

Though Tenali saved himself each time with his wit, he soon devised a plan to get rid of the death penalty once and for all.

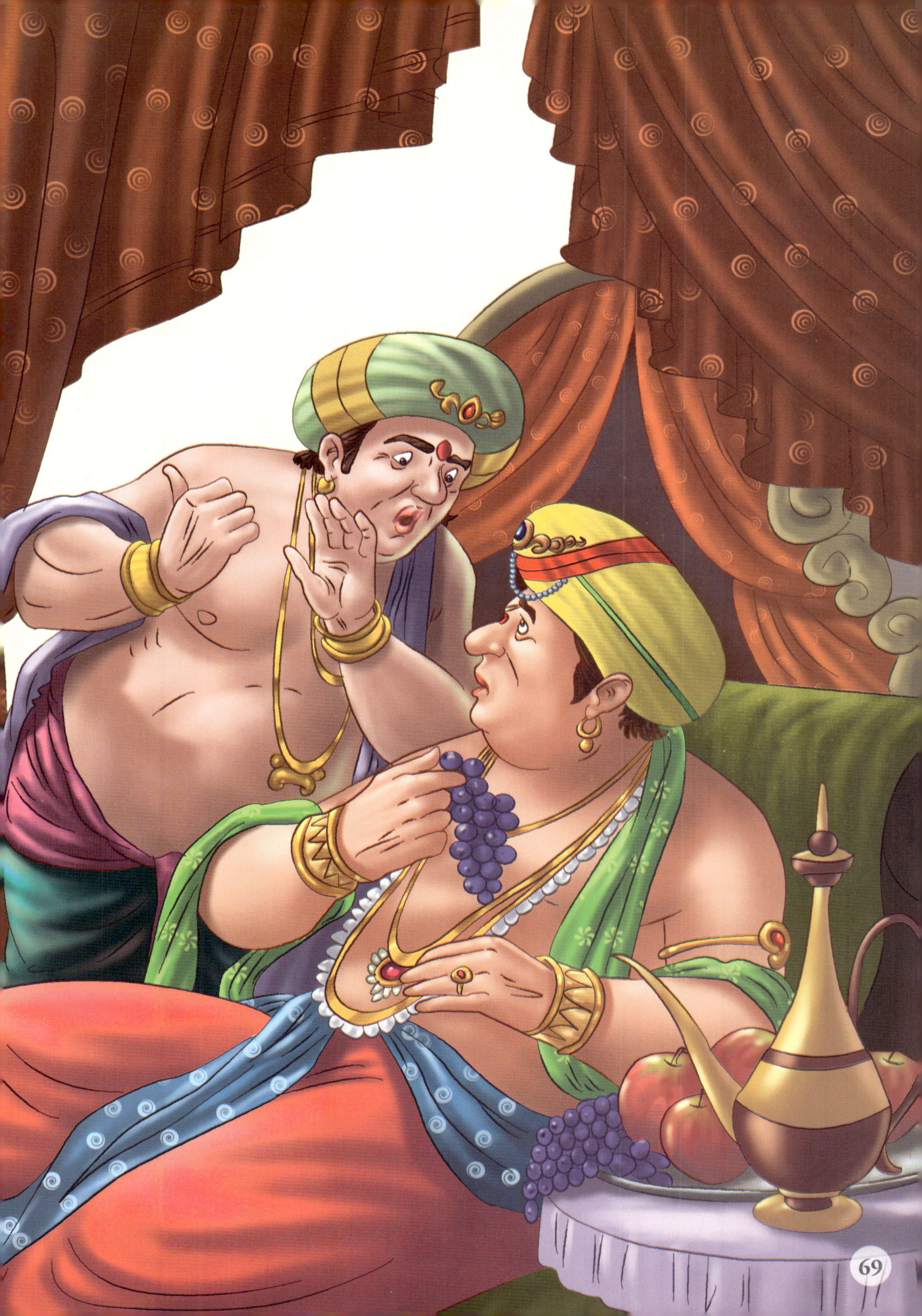

One day, he went to Thathacharya and said, "Rajguru, a famous dancer has come to town. She has heard so much about you that she wants to meet you. She has even asked you to go to her dressed as a woman so that you do not get recognised."

Thathacharya was very eager to meet this dancer and agreed to Tenali's proposal immediately. Now Tenali then went over to the king and told him the same story. King Rayalu was also very interested in meeting this beautiful dancer and agreed to go at once.

When night fell, both men, dressed as women, reached the place where Tenali had told them. Thathacharya, who had reached earlier, suddenly heard the sound of a woman's anklets. And the king, whose anklets were the ones that were making all that noise, saw a woman seated before him in the dark. Both 'women' waited for the other person to start a conversation.

Finally, Thathacharya turned around and told 'her', "Well, why don't you start with your dance?"

King Rayalu, on immediately hearing his voice, yelled, "Guruji, what are you doing here?"

Now even Thathacharya realised that he was actually in front of the king. Both men realised that they had actually been

fooled by Tenali. As they tried to find their way out in the darkness, Tenali locked the door. He then told them, "I will let both of you go, but only on one condition – you'll have to stop threatening me with the death penalty all the time."

The king and Thathacharya knew they were trapped and had no option but to agree to Tenali Rama's wish.

Death by Choice

Once upon a time, a man came to Tenali Rama's doorstep and said that he was a lost relative from his home town. Though unable to recognise him, Tenali allowed him to stay in his house for some time.

Little did he realise that this man was actually a spy from a neighbouring kingdom, who had come with the objective of killing King Sri Krishna Deva Rayalu.

Now Tenali Rama had to go out of town for some time. Finding this to be a golden opportunity, the spy decided to carry out his mission immediately. He sent a note to the king in the handwriting of Tenali's wife. It said, "Please come to my house immediately. I am very unwell and my husband is out of town. I need medical attention."

As soon as the king got this message, he rushed out. As he entered the house, the spy attacked him, but the king was able to save himself and the spy was arrested.

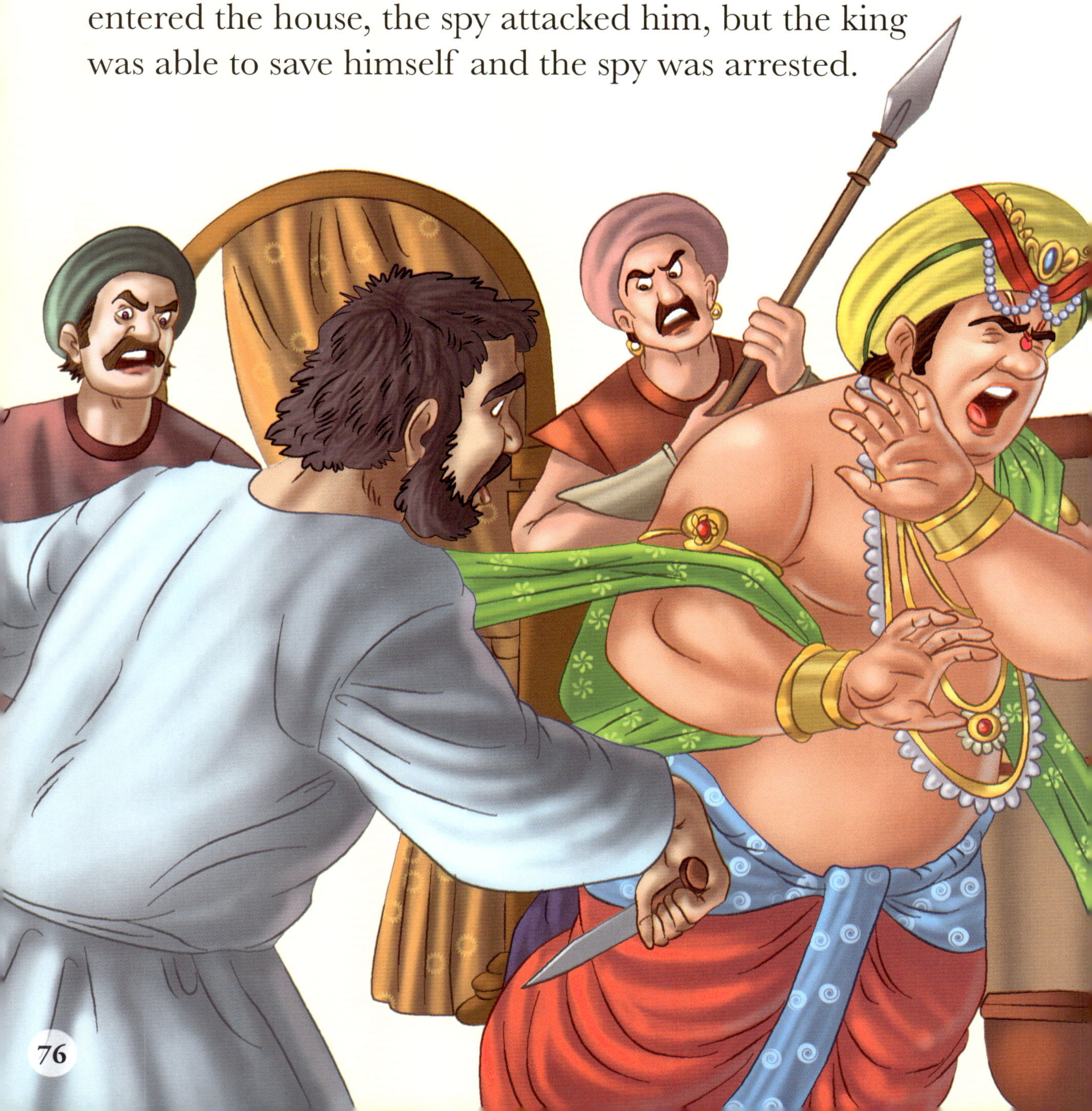

On his return, Tenali was summoned to court. The king was beside himself with rage. He told Tenali, "This is unpardonable! You let a spy stay in your house? He was planning to kill me! For this, you will be executed. Please let me know how you would like to die..."

Tenali heard what the king had to say and said, "My lord, I would like to die in my old age."

Hearing this, the whole court, including the king broke into peals of laughter. Needless to say, Tenali Rama's life was spared.

A Heavy Debt

Tenali Rama had once taken some money from King Sri Krishna Deva Rayalu as a loan. Soon it was time for him to repay the money. But Tenali had no intention of paying the money back. He kept thinking about a suitable way to avoid payment and finally hit upon a brilliant idea.

One day, the king received a note from Tenali's wife, where she said that her husband was extremely ill and wanted to see the king immediately. Though king decided to go to Tenali at once, at the back of his mind he had guessed that Tenali was perhaps trying to get out of paying any money.

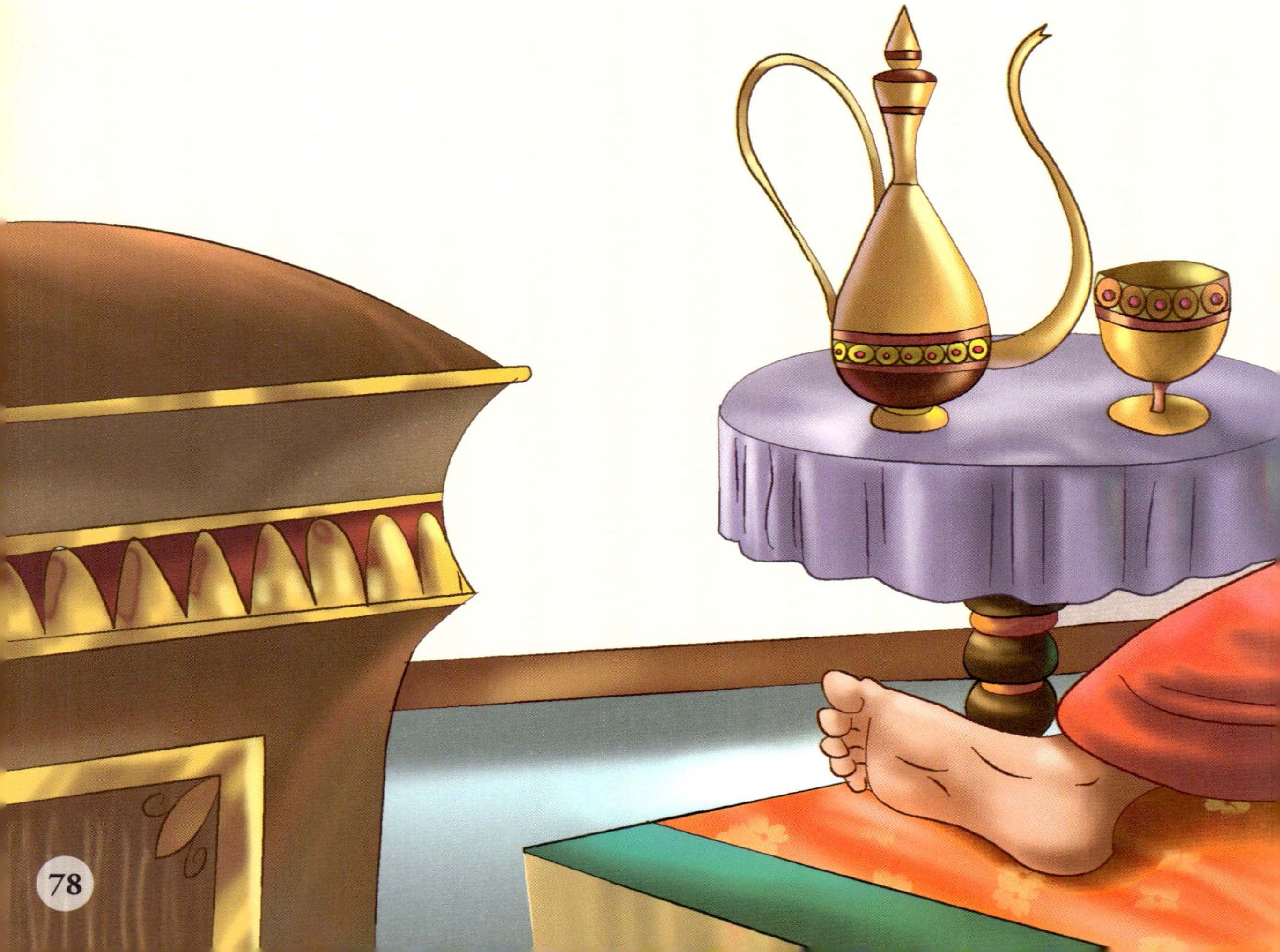

As he reached Tenali's house, the king was appalled to see his beloved court poet lying in bed. He was extremely sad as he watched Tenali writhe in pain. He asked his wife, "What is the matter with him? What is ailing him so?"

Tenali Rama's wife informed him, "My Lord, it is the burden of your loan. It has pulled him down completely and now he cannot get up any more."

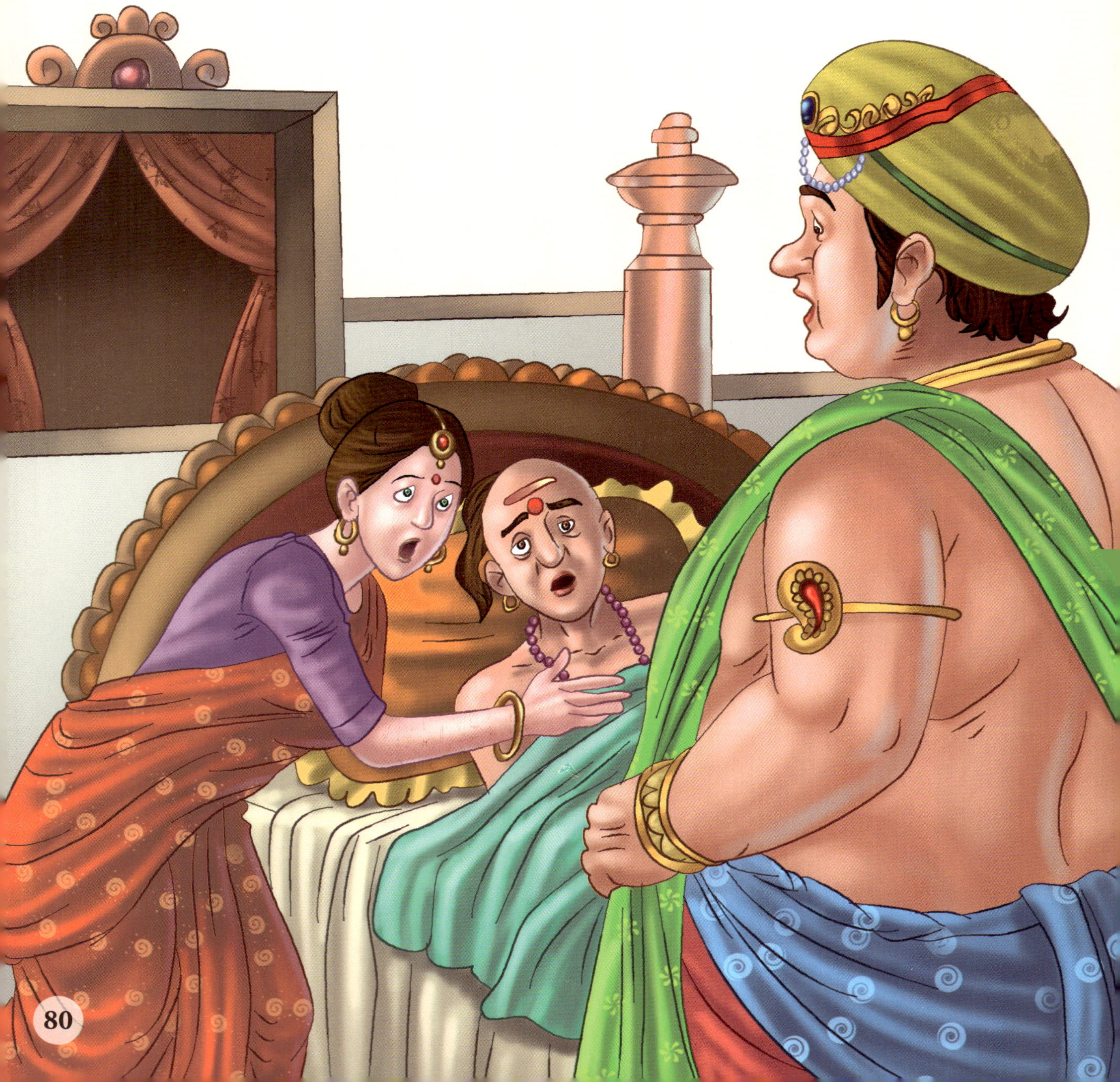

Hearing this, King Rayalu immediately said, "My friend, there is no need for you to feel this way. You do not have to pay me anything. I am calling off the debt that you owed me. Please stop worrying and get back on your feet once again."

Hearing this, Tenali threw off his blanket and jumped out of the bed. The king was surprised at Tenali's actions and soon caught on to his plan. He said, "Tenali? What is the meaning of this? You did this to get out of paying me the money? You lied to me?"

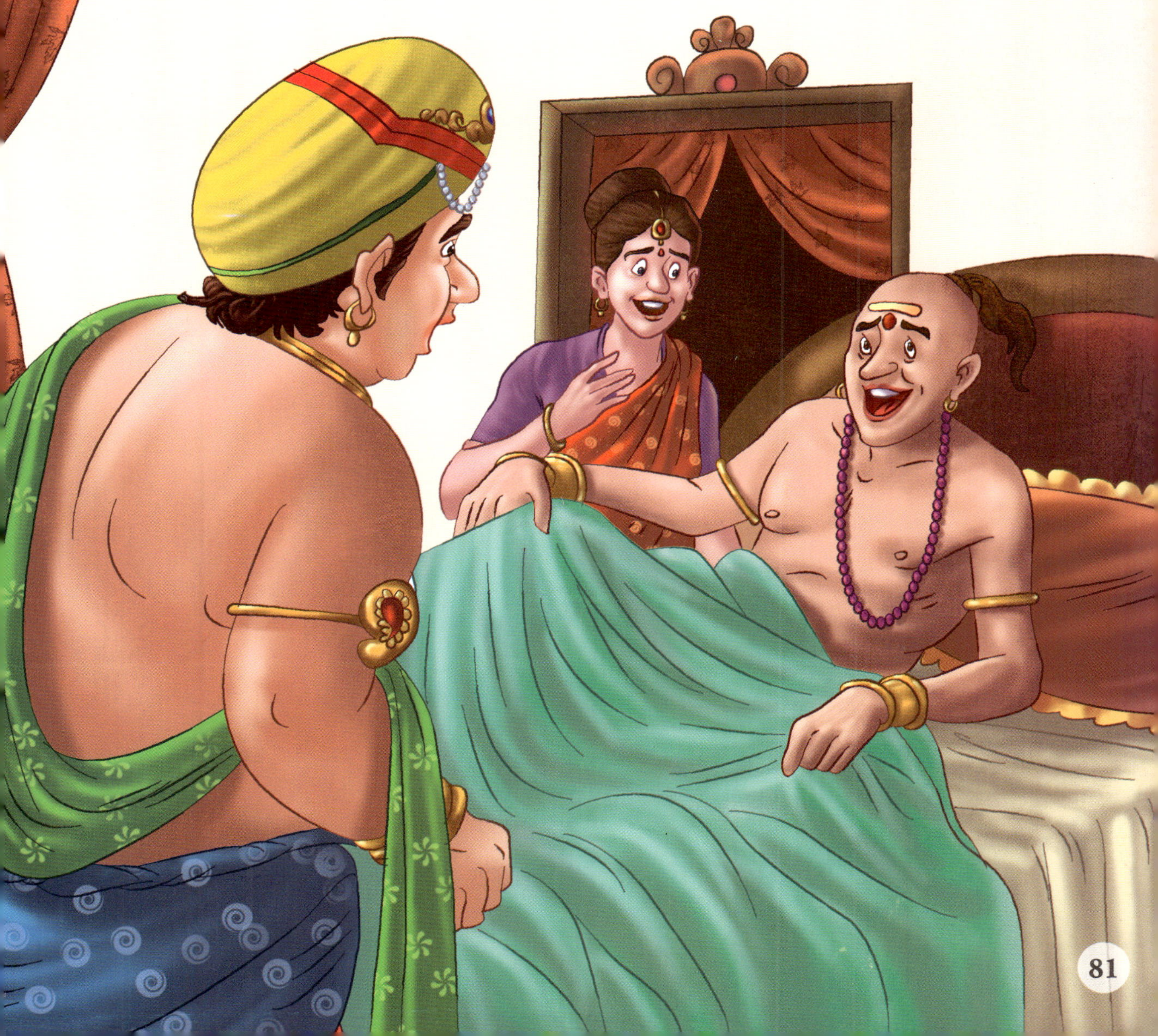

Tenali very simply replied, "No your Majesty, I did not lie. I was really under the burden of your debt and therefore was unable to get out of bed. Now that you have lifted that burden, I am well again. Do you still think that I was lying, O noble King?"

The king was amazed at Tenali's sharp wit and burst out into roars of laughter.

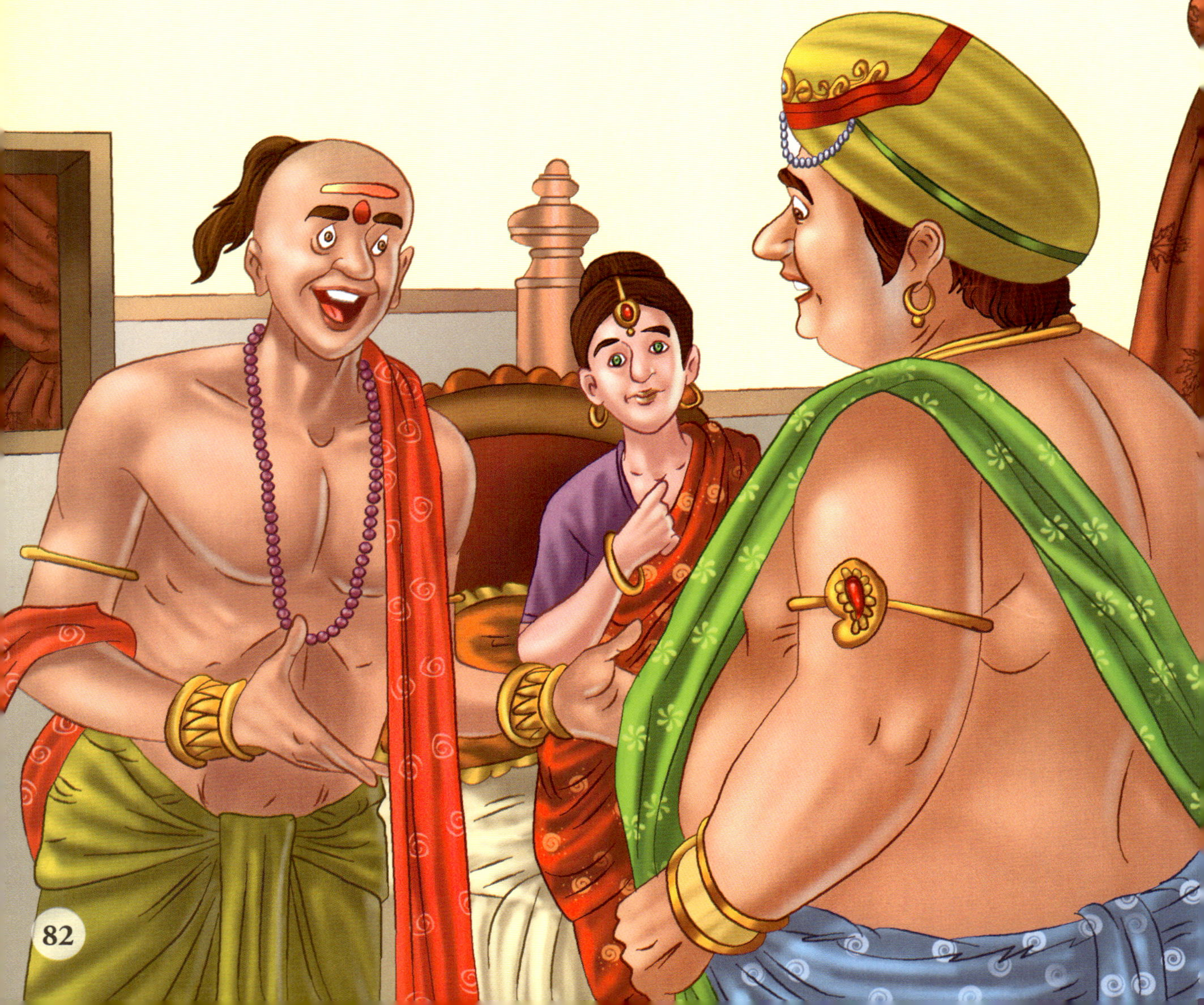

The Real Culprit

One day, in the court of King Sri Krishna Deva Rayalu of Vijaynagar, the court had assembled as usual. As they were discussing the matters of the state, a shepherd ran in and fell before the feet of the king. His voice trembled as he said, "My Lord, I have come to you for justice."

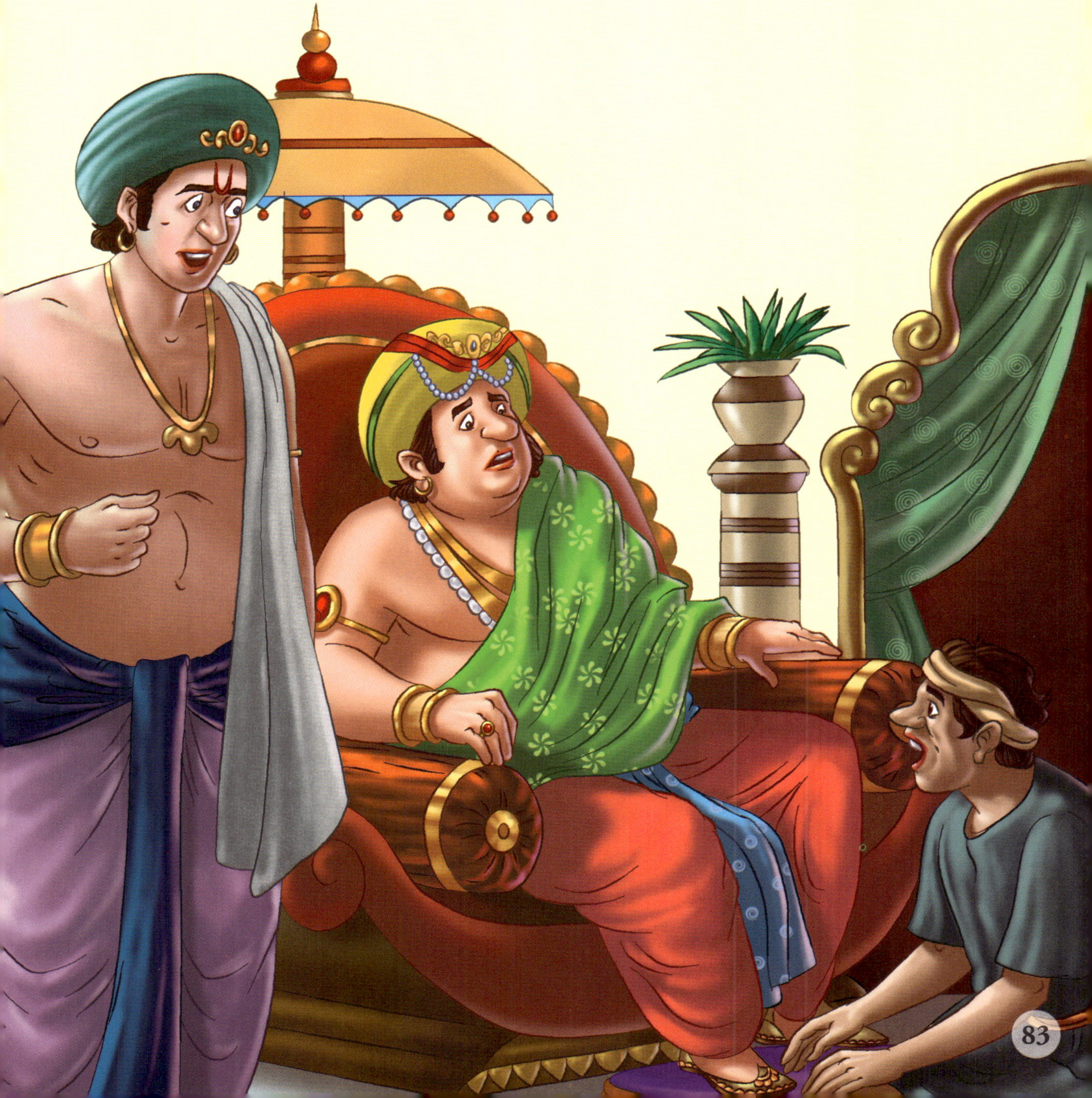

The king was amazed at what was happening. He picked the shepherd up and asked, "Please tell me what is the matter first."

The shepherd, between sobs, said, "My Lord, my neighbour is an old miser. He never paid any money to repair his old walls and yesterday it finally crashed, killing my goat beneath it. Please ask him to compensate me for my loss."

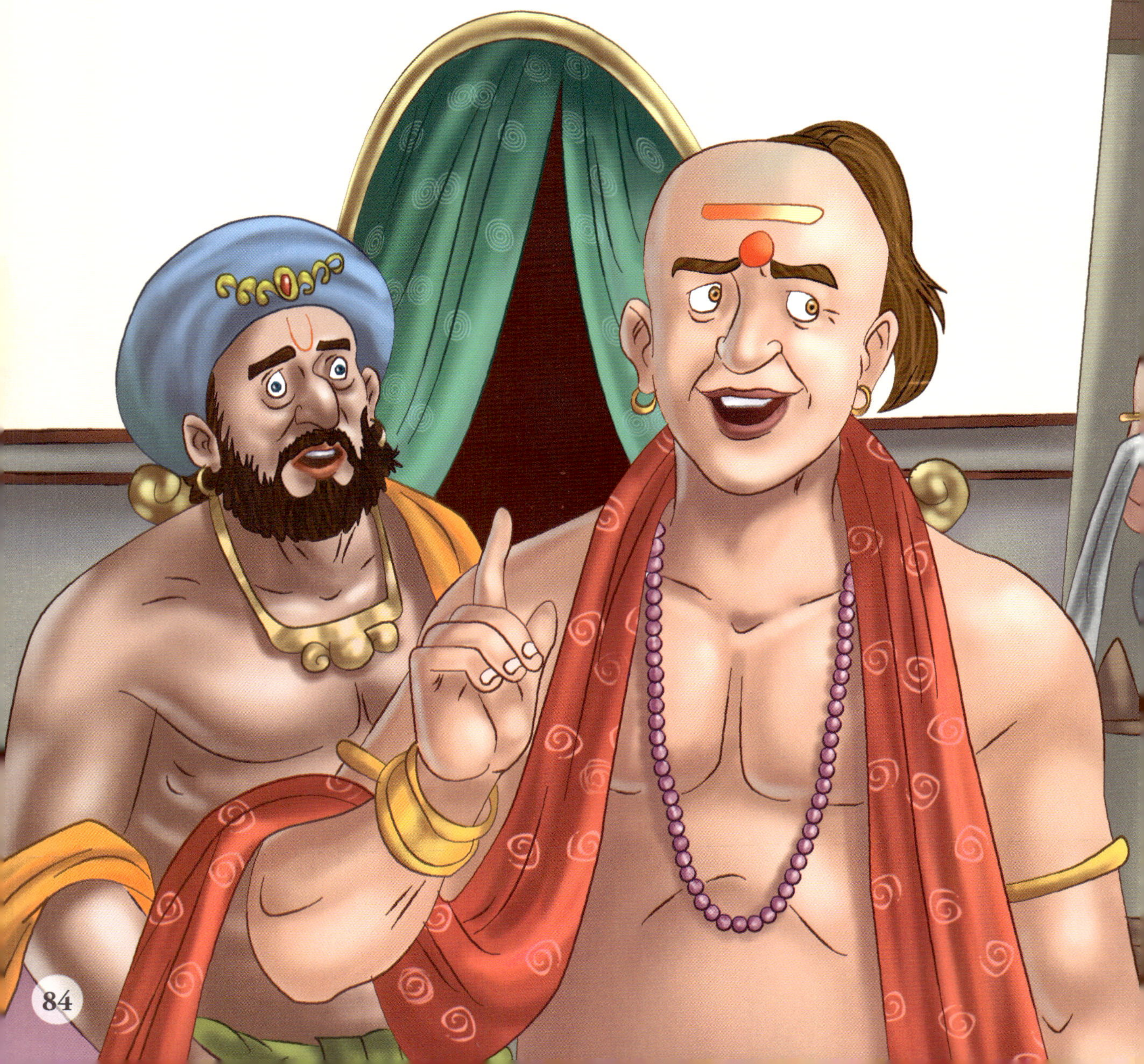

As the shepherd left after the king assured him that he would look into the matter himself, Tenali Rama got up from his seat and told the king, "Sire, please give me some time. I feel there is more to this case than what the shepherd is saying. I will investigate and unravel the real culprit before you."

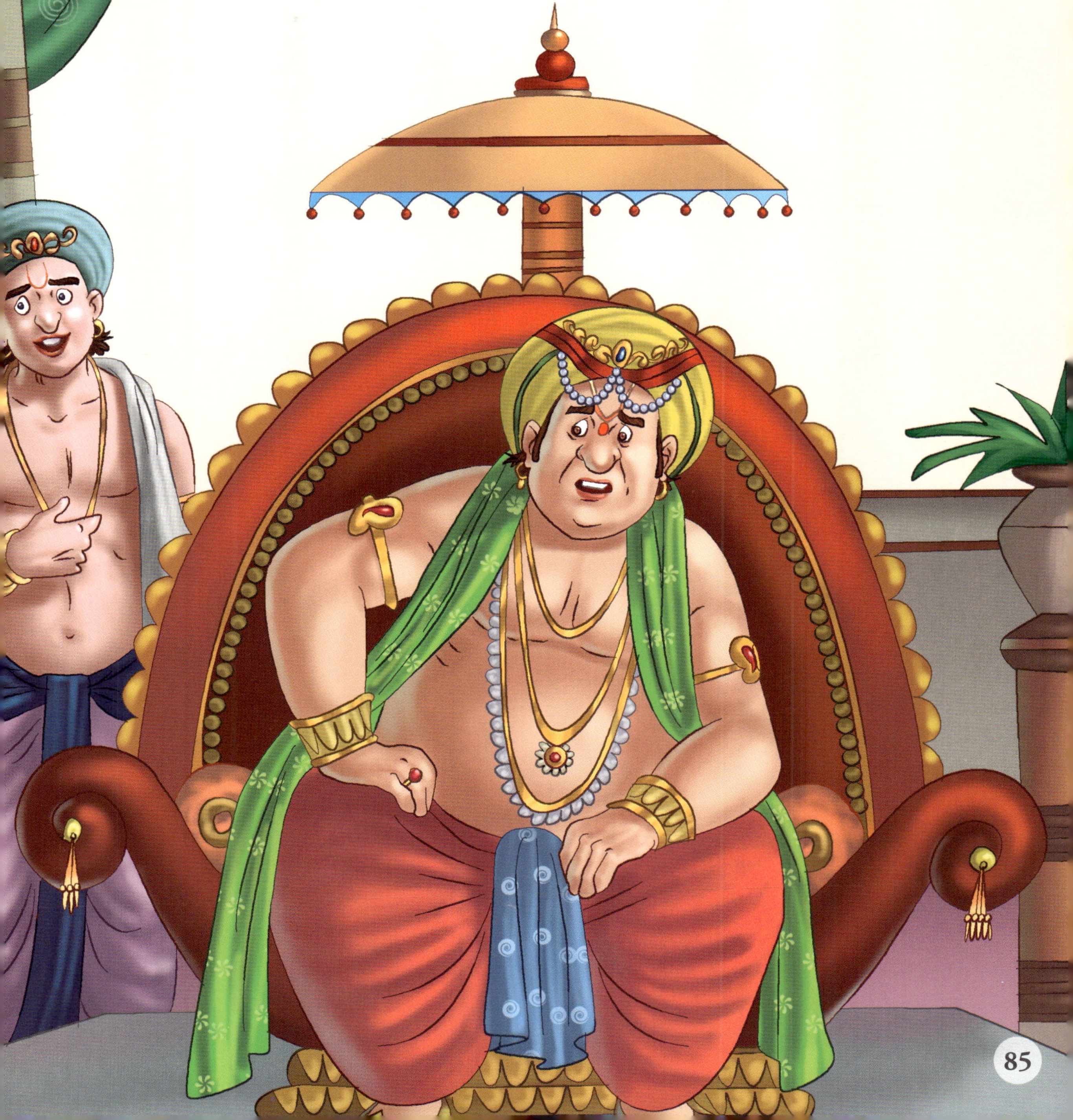

With the king's consent, Tenali Rama first summoned the neighbour of the shepherd. On hearing the charge, he promptly replied, "My lord, the blame does not rest with me. I hired a mason who, as it turns out, did not do a good job. He is the one responsible for the shepherd's loss."

On hearing that, Tenali called the mason to court. He in turn specified that he had hired a labourer to mix the cement. According to him, it was the labourer's fault that the cement did not stick.

So it was the labourer's turn to be summoned to court next. He in turn said, "It is not me Sir, it is the man who brought the water. He is the one to blame. He poured more water than what was required and therefore the cement mixture was not strong enough. Please catch him!"

After the cement-mixer left, the man who had added the water came before Tenali. On hearing the accusation, he turned around and said, "Sir, the water carrier that I used was too big. It carried more water than what it should have. You must apprehend the shopkeeper who sold it to me."

Now it was the turn of the shopkeeper. He made it clear that instead of holding him responsible, Tenali Rama should question the man who sold that water carrier to him. Tenali asked the shopkeeper to send that man to him immediately.

Lo and behold, it was the shepherd who came back before Tenali Rama. The shopkeeper pointed to him and said, "Sir, he sold me the water carrier."

Tenali Rama looked at the shepherd and said, "Look what happens when you do not work properly One day, it all comes back to you. I am sorry my friend, but your goat died because of your own fault. No one owes you any compensation."

As the shepherd left the court, King Rayalu turned to Tenali Rama and said, "Well done, my friend, well done!"

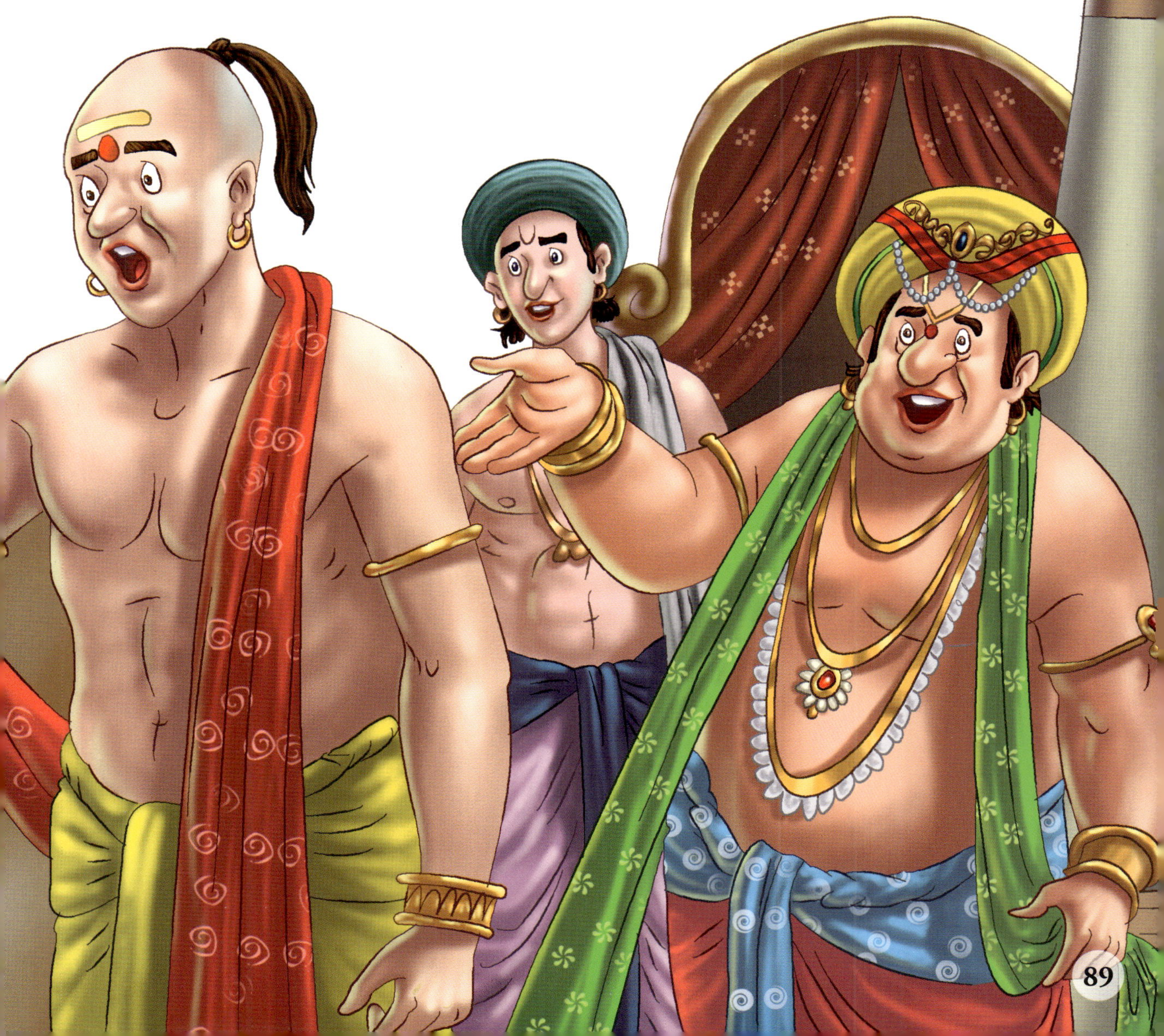

Lies, Lies

One day, a priest came into the court of King Sri Krishna Deva Rayalu at Vijayanagar. After greeting the king and all the members of court who were present there, he said, “My Lord, I hear that the greatest minds of Vijayanagar are seated here. In which case, I want to ask a question and I want a satisfactory answer from one of your ministers. Will you permit me to ask?”

King Rayalu obviously could not back away from this proposal. He turned to the priest and said, "You may proceed. Rajguru Thathacharya here will be happy to answer your question."

The man then turned to the Rajguru and said, "My Lord, can you prove to me that all that is around us is actually maya?"

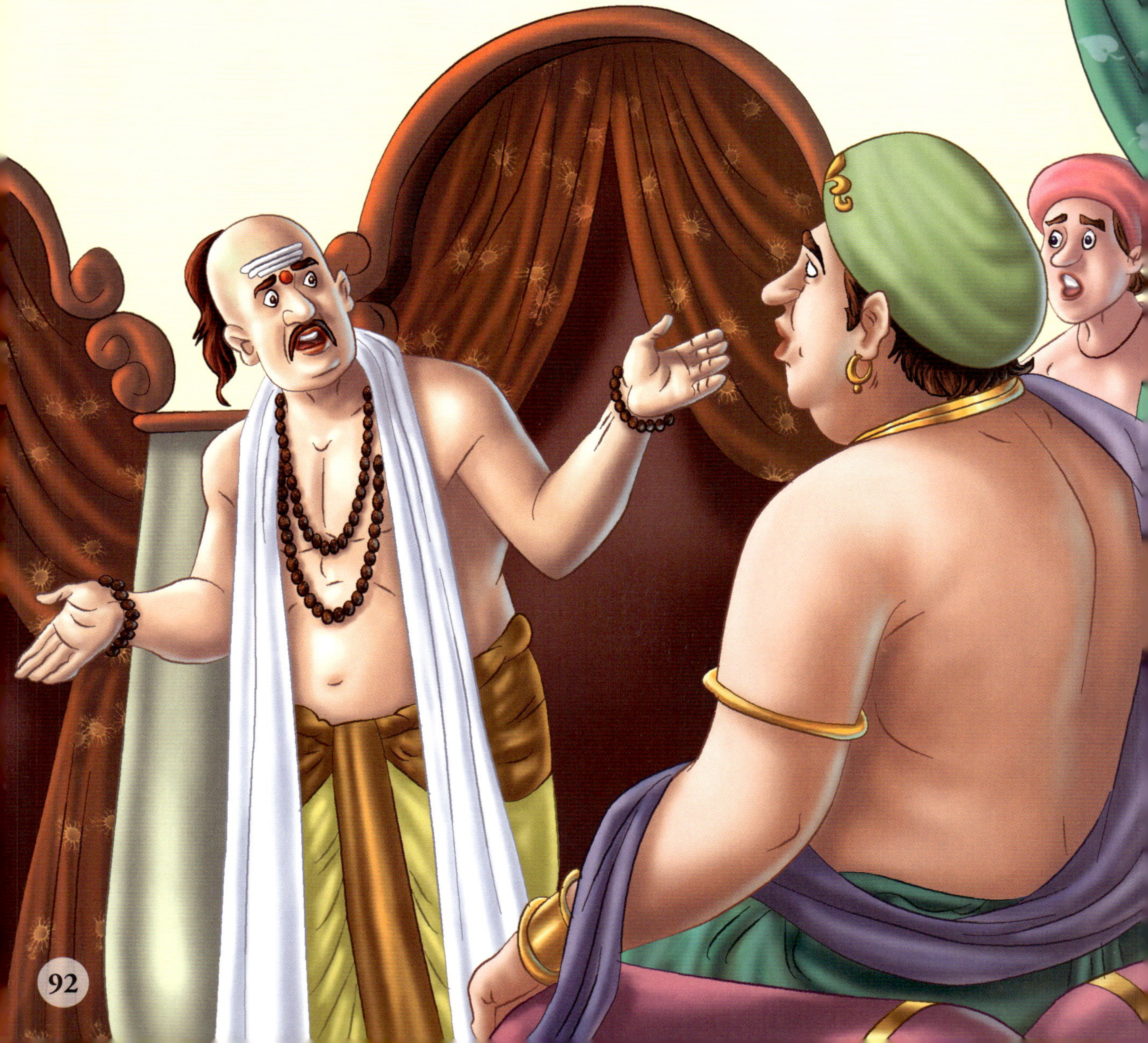

Thathacharya smiled at the man and replied, "Of course, my friend... After all, this is written in the shashtras, is it not?"

The man was not convinced. He said, "That is not a suitable answer, My Lord. That is mainly theoretical. I wanted a more practical answer to my question."

Thathacharya was quick to reply again. He said, "Well my friend, let me elaborate. See, when we come to this world, we come with nothing. Then, when we die, we leave without any of our worldly possessions. Therefore, all that we acquire in this life is false. You could say all that is maya."

The priest was still not happy with what Thathacharya had to say. He turned to King Rayalu and said, "My Lord, I am sure that you will agree with me that Rajguru is giving us an answer which is not practical. Can anyone else here satisfy me?"

On hearing the priest's demands, the king turned to Tenali Rama. On having the king's approval Tenali immediately got up and said, "To answer your question my friend, I first need to ask you a question. Where would you say are the Himalayas?"

The man quickly replied, "Why, they are to the north."

Tenali then said, "Right. And where would a person in China say the Himalayas are?"

Again the man replied, "To the south."

“Correct, then both answers will be correct? Or as I can also say, both answers are wrong. And not just in this case. Even in matters like day and night, both answers may be correct, or wrong. So nothing is true. Everything is a lie. Or, answering your question, everything is maya.”

The priest had to concede that Tenali Rama had answered his question with the most practical examples. King Rayalu smiled at Tenali as he had once again saved the honour of Vijayanagar.

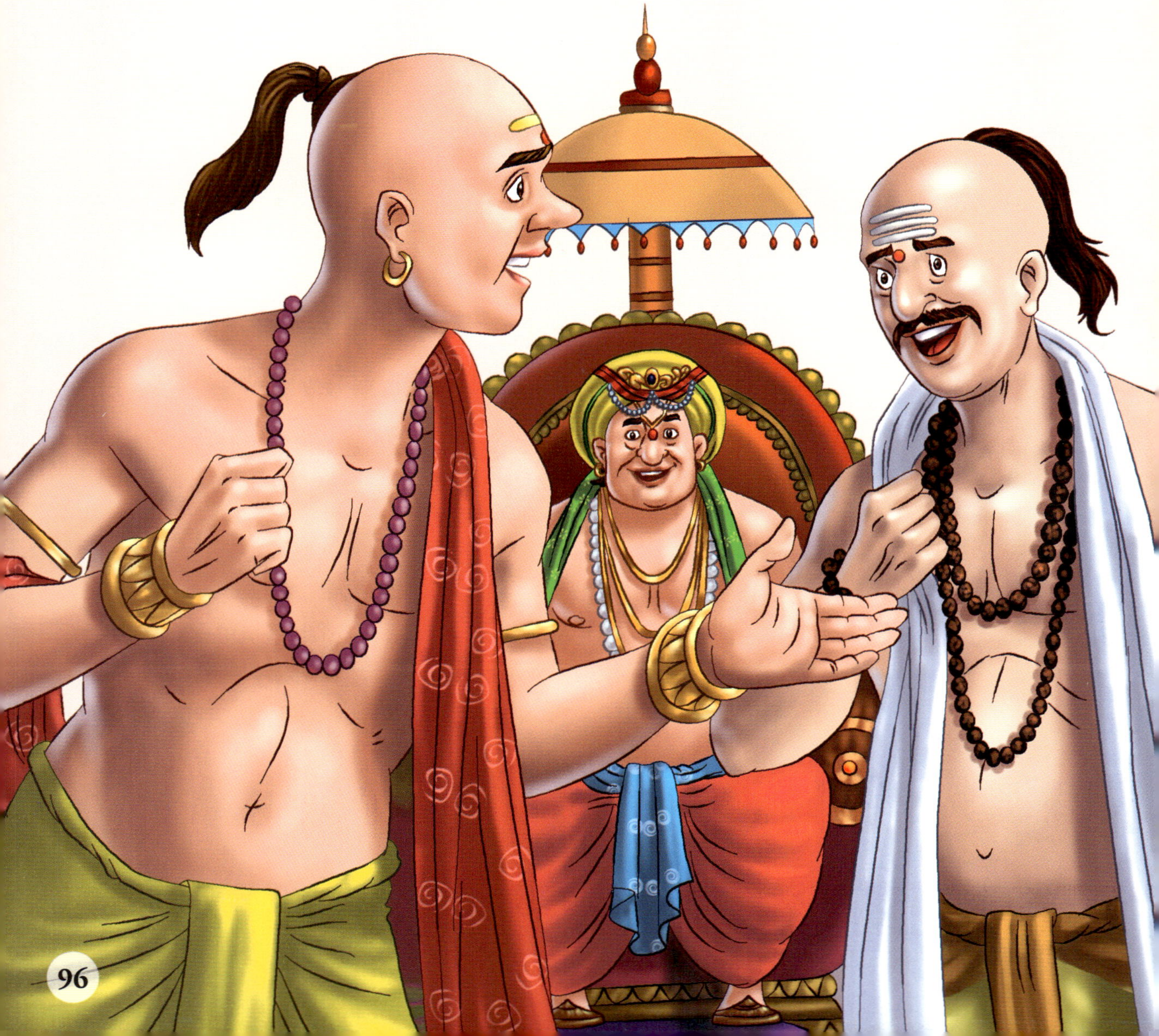

Honesty

Rajguru Thathacharya once suggested to King Sri Krishna Deva Rayalu that as compared to rich people, the poor were more dishonest. He added that this was definitely because the poor lied more out of necessity.

Tenali Rama was quick to object to the Rajguru's point. To settle the argument, he asked the king for two bags of gold and, some time. As the king handed him the bags, he went to a place which he knew was frequented by a rich merchant and a poor man every day. He left the two bags there and went back to the palace.

As was expected, the merchant found one bag while walking through that path in the morning. He took the bag and considering it to be a boon from Goddess Lakshmi he went home and kept the money.

Within the course of the day, the poor man also found the other bag. But instead of taking it away with him, he went straight to the royal treasury and handed the bag over to the treasury officials.

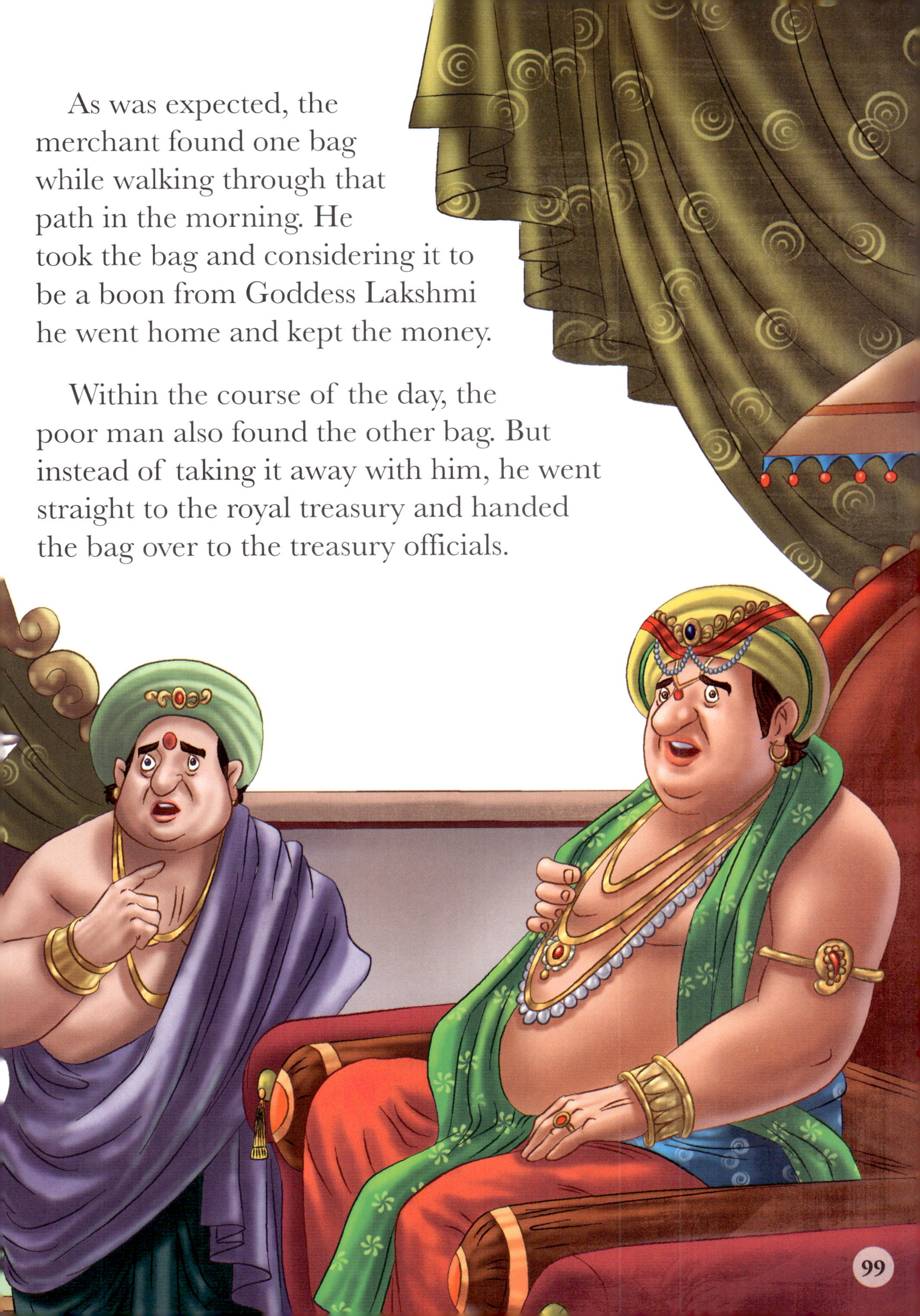

Next day, as the court assembled, Tenali Rama walked up to the king and declared that only one bag had been returned and contrary to what the Rajguru had said, it was the poor man who had returned the bag. The king immediately summoned both the merchant and the poor man.

When questioned, the merchant replied, "Sir, I considered the money to be a boon from Goddess Lakshmi and therefore took it with me. However, I invested the money and lost it all. I am ruined."

The king then turned to the poor man and asked him why he returned the bag, especially since he could have used it himself. The poor man replied, "Your Majesty, that bag did not belong to me. I thought that perhaps the bag belonged to someone who needed the money more than me. Therefore, I came to the treasury and returned it."

The king smiled at Tenali Rama, who had once again proved his point satisfactorily. Rajguru Thathacharya was however nowhere to be seen.

Faults

One day in the court of King Sri Krishna Deva Rayalu of Vijaynagar, Rajguru Thathacharya got into a heated argument with one of the courtiers. The courtier had claimed that while people criticise others easily, they never point out to the faults in their own self. Rajguru obviously disagreed with this.

As the argument progressed, a painter arrived at the court. He said that as a tribute to King Rayalu, he had drawn the portrait of a woman. The king was extremely impressed by the painting, but as he passed it on to his courtiers, they all started pointing out some or the other flaws. No one was completely satisfied with it.

Tenali Rama then came up to the king and said, “My Lord, I have an idea. Why don’t you hang that picture in the centre of the city? We will post a banner there which will instruct people to mark the portion in the painting which they think is not correct!”

The king agreed to Rama’s proposition. Next evening, when the picture came back to the palace after display in the city, the king was horrified to see that there were so many marks on it that the actual picture had disappeared.

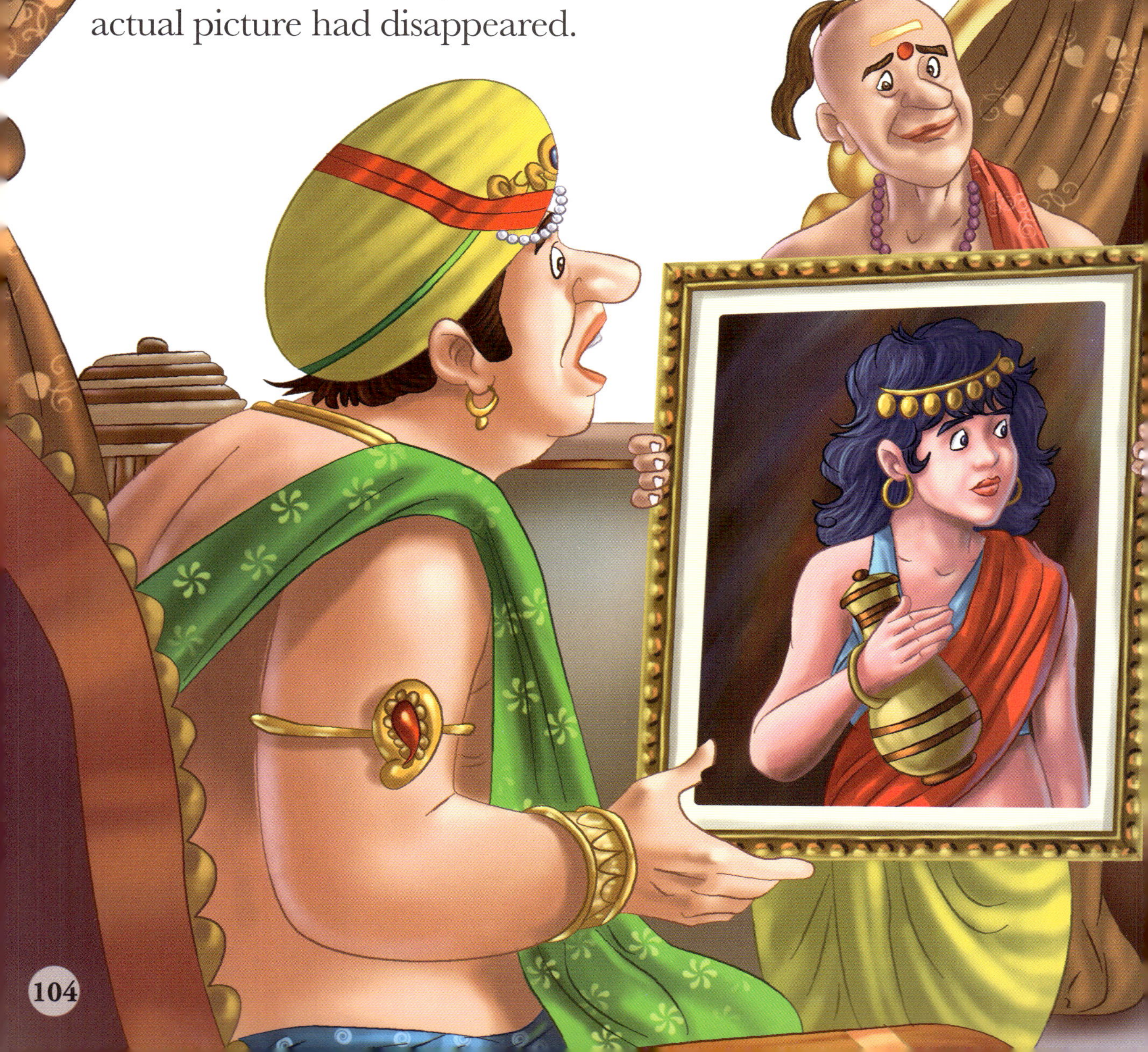

On seeing the king's face, Rama went up to him and said, "Now tomorrow let us put this picture up at the same place and tell people to rectify whatever they think is wrong in it. There will of course be a reward for everyone who does that."

Again, when the picture came back in the evening, the king was horrified to see that though a reward was offered, no one had even bothered to touch the painting. Rama then turned to the king and said, "People like to point out flaws, but they never bother to correct them."

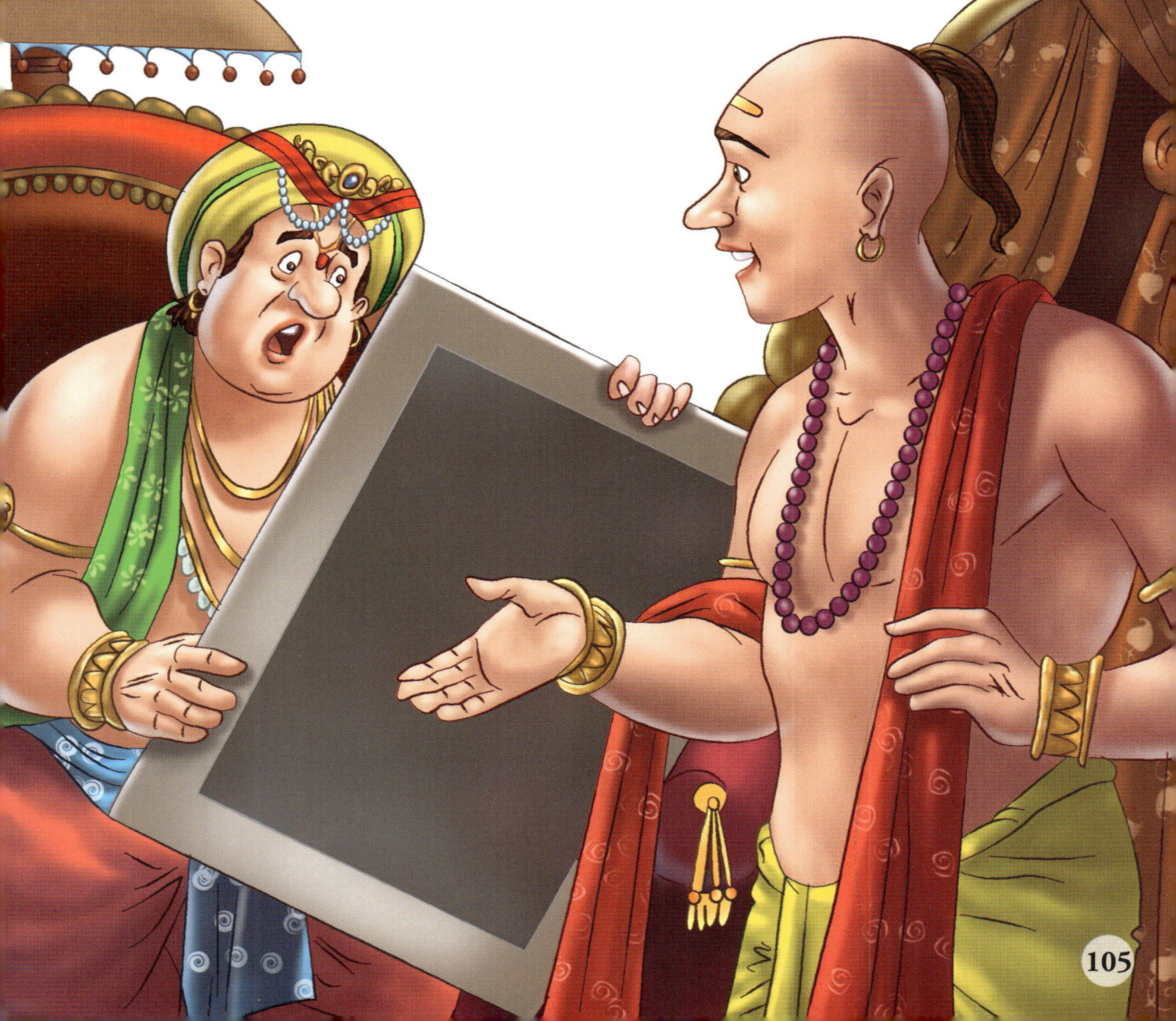

The courtier who was arguing with Thathacharya, the day before, was trying hard not to break into peals of laughter. The king simply rewarded Tenali Rama for proving his point. And, the painter was handsomely rewarded too.

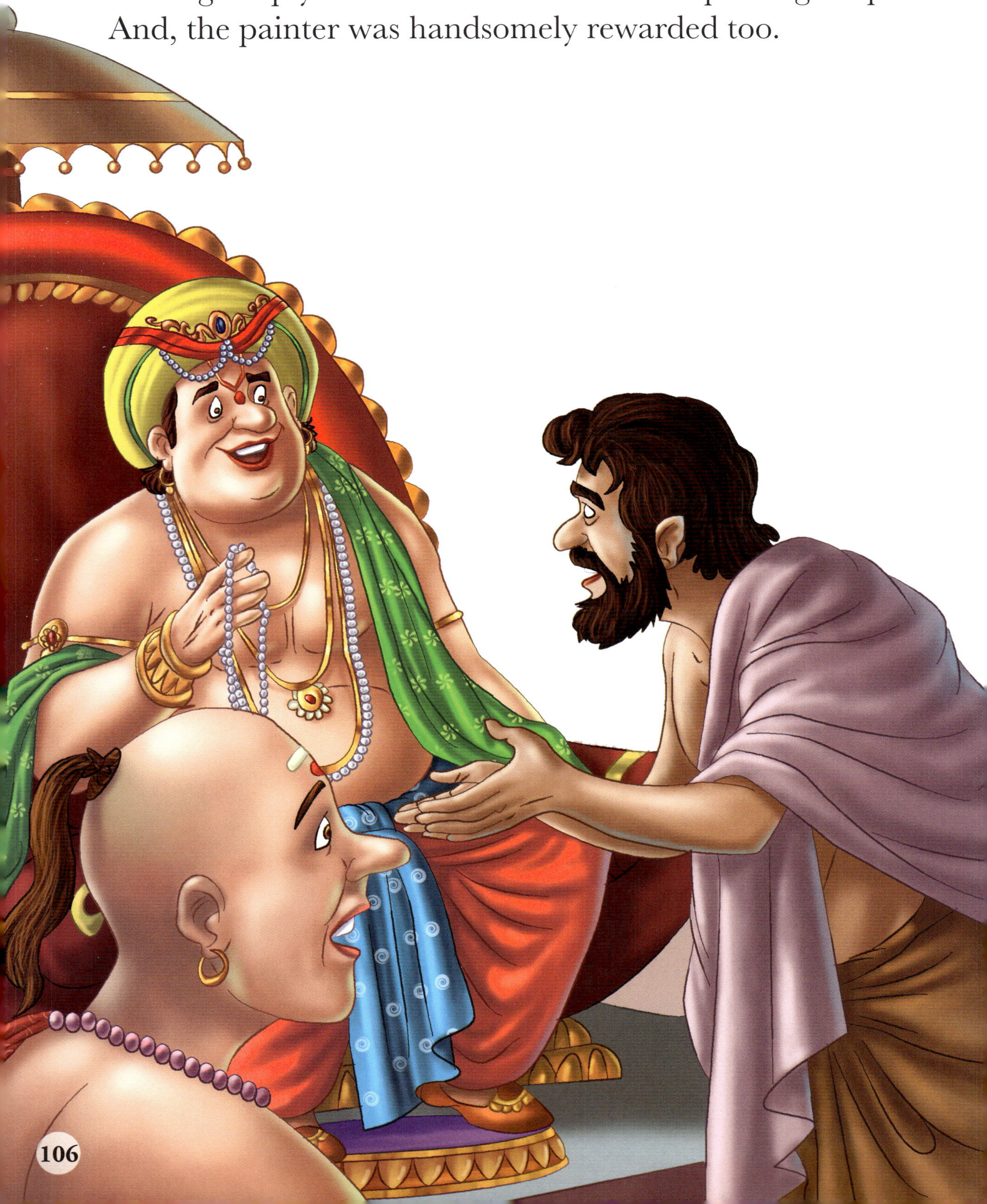

The Royal Brinjal

King Sri Krishna Deva Rayalu was very proud of his vegetable garden. He had hired the very best gardeners to tend to it every day. He was also very strict about people taking vegetables from this garden. If anyone were ever found guilty of stealing from this garden, the king would inflict the death penalty on them.

Now one day, Tenali Rama's son had gone to the palace. As his father was busy with his court duties, Rama's son was busy roaming around in the palace. Soon he came into the vegetable garden. Not being able to resist himself, he plucked a brinjal from a plant and carried it home with him. Tenali's wife too, not knowing where the vegetable had come from, cooked it immediately. When Tenali finally had it for dinner, he knew at once where the brinjal had come from. On asking his son, his worst fears were realised.

Now Tenali was in a bit of a fix. In the event the king would find out, Tenali would have to ask his son to lie, which he could not do. Neither could he tell the king that his son was the real culprit behind the theft of the brinjal. Some of the ministers in court who were jealous of Tenali came to know of it and decided to inform the king so that Tenali would be in trouble.

Tenali thought hard over the matter and finally came up with a solution. As his son lay asleep in the terrace at night, Tenali sneaked up behind him and dumped a pail of water over him.

Next day, the king summoned Tenali to court and questioned him about the missing brinjal. Tenali categorically denied his son's involvement in the theft. The jealous ministers, wanting to put the last nail in the coffin for Tenali, asked the king to bring his son to court and ask him. The king too knew that Tenali would never encourage his son to lie and therefore agreed to the idea.

When Tenali's son came to court, the king asked him whether he had taken a brinjal from the vegetable garden. His son innocently answered that he had. Just as the king was about to reprimand Tenali for it, Tenali put his plan into action.

" Sir, he is a young boy. He does not know what he is agreeing to. He is just saying things," said Tenali.

The king had a doubt that Tenali was trying to shield his son's actions and said, "Your son has agreed to his crime, Tenali. You cannot talk your way out of this now."

"If that be the case, please also ask him another question. Why don't you ask him whether it rained last night?"

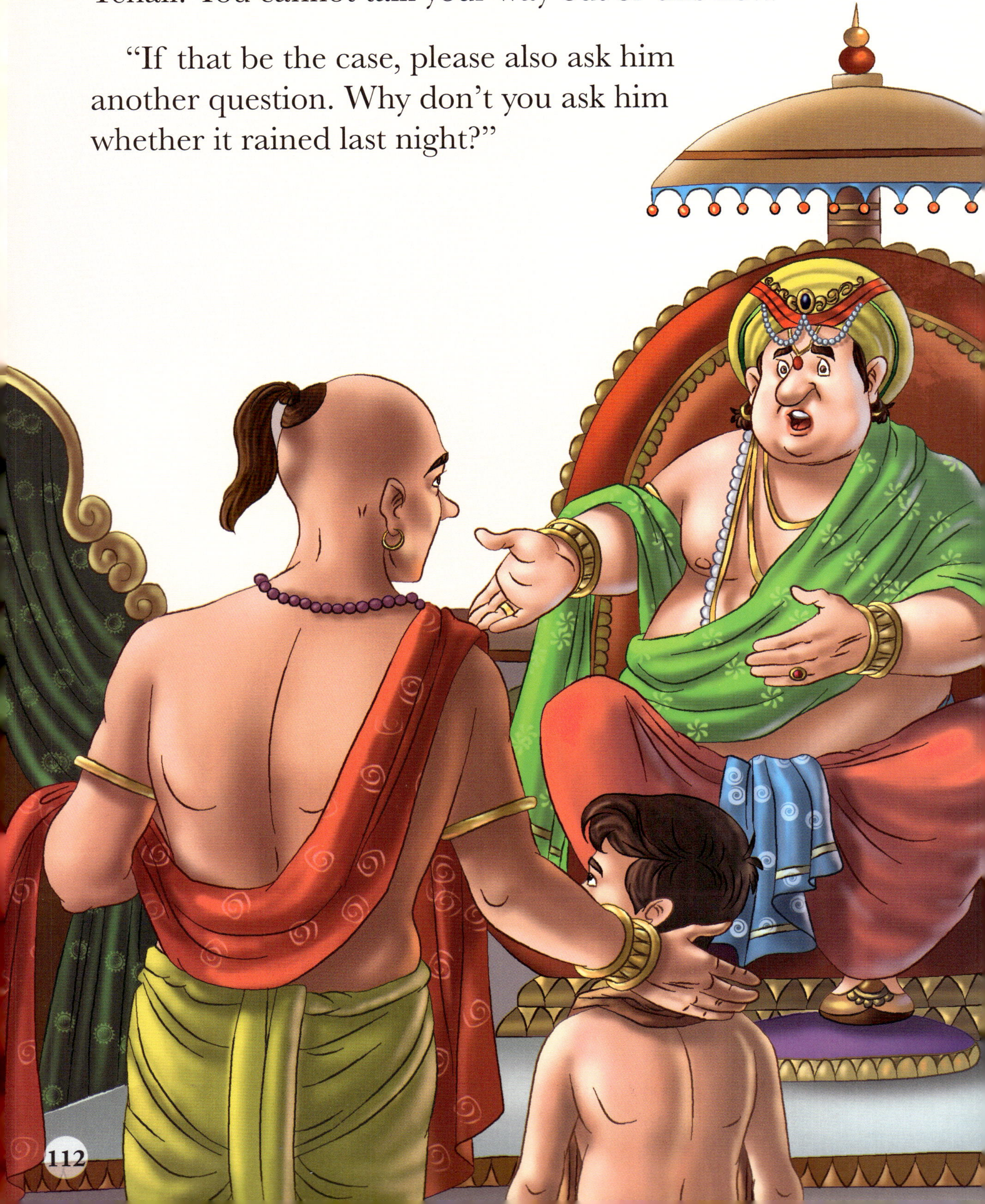

Thinking that this time Tenali could not find a way to escape, the king asked Tenali's son the same question. As he had been drenched last night while sleeping, the boy replied yes to this question as well. Now everyone knew that it had in fact not rained last night.

Tenali then said, "Now do you see what I mean My Lord? He has no clue as to what you are asking him. My son would never take anything without asking me. Now, do you still believe that he is the thief?"

The king had no other option but to accept Tenali's story. He apologised and asked his men to keep searching for the thief.

The Content Man's Gift

One day, King Sri Krishna Deva Rayalu saw Tenali Rama come to court wearing some of his finest clothes. Surprised as seeing Tenali in clothes other than his saffron shawl, King Rayalu asked him, "Tenali, what is the matter? How come you are wearing these clothes today? Is it some kind of a special occasion?"

Tenali shyly replied, "Your Majesty, after working in your court for so long, I have been able to save quite some money. Therefore I decided to buy some nice clothes for a change."

King Rayalu smiled and said, "Well then Tenali, now that you have amassed a lot of wealth, I think you should give something to the poor and needy people."

Tenali abruptly replied, "My Lord, I said that I have saved some money. To start distributing my wealth, I will have to wait for some more time."

"Come on now Tenali, do not try to be a miser. Build a lavish house and give it away to people who really need it. I am sure you are kind enough to do that."

Tenali now had no option but to agree to the king's suggestion and confirmed that he would indeed do as King Rayalu said.

Within some time, Tenali built a magnificent house and fitted it with all the luxuries that a house could provide. After that he put a board in front of the house which said, "This house will be given to the man who is content with everything in his life."

Every day, people would come and stare at the house, but they did not have the courage to go and tell Tenali that they were content with everything that they had in their life. They knew that the intelligent Tenali would soon expose their lie.

One day however, a poor man was crossing the house and he too saw the board hanging there. He immediately walked over to Tenali and said, "My Lord, I have read the board that you have placed outside your new house. I would like to inform you that I am content with everything that I have in my life. Therefore, I think that the new house should belong to me."

Tenali answered so quickly that it almost seemed that he had an answer prepared. He said, "Well, if you are content with everything that you have in your life, I don't think you need anything else. Otherwise you would not be content – right?"

The poor man had no option but to concede to Tenali's statement.

Finally, Tenali went to King Rayalu and told him that no one had come forward to claim his house. Believing him, the king asked him what he planned to do with it? Tenali humbly said that, since no one had claimed it, he planned to move into it himself and start living there.

Birth of the Vessels

There was once a greedy money lender in Vijaynagar, who would lend money to the poor people, but charge them a huge interest for it. Soon this news came to Tenali Rama, who then decided to teach this man a lesson.

He went to the moneylender and asked him whether he could borrow three vessels from him as he had to prepare a huge feast for some people. The moneylender agreed, but obviously charged Tenali two gold coins for each vessel. Instead of arguing with him, Tenali agreed immediately.

He then went to the market where he bought three more vessels of the same shape but much smaller in size. The next day he went back to the moneylender and said, "Here are your three vessels. They gave birth to these other three vessels when they were with me. So I have brought them back with their mothers. Please do take care of them."

The moneylender had overjoyed when he received six vessels instead of three. He agreed to what Tenali had to say.

Within the next few days, Tenali went back to the moneylender and told him that he needed another lot of vessels for another feast. While the moneylender gave him all the vessels that he needed, he told him, "Please be careful, these vessels are pregnant too. Please be very careful with them."

Now Tenali was supposed to return with the vessels in three days' time. But he was missing. Furious, the moneylender landed at Tenali's house and demanded that he give back his vessels immediately.

Tenali calmly replied, “I am sorry, but your vessels died at childbirth. I tried my level best, but I could not save them.”

The moneylender began to argue with Tenali that it was not possible for them to die at childbirth as vessels could not have babies. Tenali then told him to come to court where the matter could be decided once and for all.

The judge on hearing both stories replied, "But you did agree the first time that the vessels had babies. Therefore, if you could accept that amazing fact that your vessels had babies the first time, you should also agree to the fact they could also die at childbirth."

The moneylender was completely helpless and he left court with a long face. He should have known that he would not be able to fight a battle of wits with Tenali Rama!

The Holy Parrot

One day, a hunter caught a beautiful parrot in the forests of Vijayanagar. Unable to kill the pretty bird, he decided to hand it over to the king as a gift. The king was extremely happy on seeing the beautiful bird. He kept it in a golden cage and fed him the best seeds and sweets that he could get in his kingdom. Even the queen was fascinated by the parrot and she too spent a lot of time with it.

Eventually, they were able to teach the bird how to say "Hare Krishna". They then started to believe that the parrot was indeed a holy parrot.

One day, when Tenali Rama came to the king's chamber to offer the prasad from the morning prayers, he found the king and the queen busy with the parrot. As they saw Tenali, they said, "Ah! I see that you have come from the temple. But look here Tenali… our parrot is more religious than you. He speaks only holy words." So saying the king asked the parrot to say Hare Krishna, which the parrot did.

Tenali was furious at the king's childish talk. He said, "My Lord, it is not because of his religious attitude, but because of what you teach him that he says those words. I am sure that in dfferent situations he will utter different words." The king and the queen were upset at what Tenali had to say and dared him to prove his point.

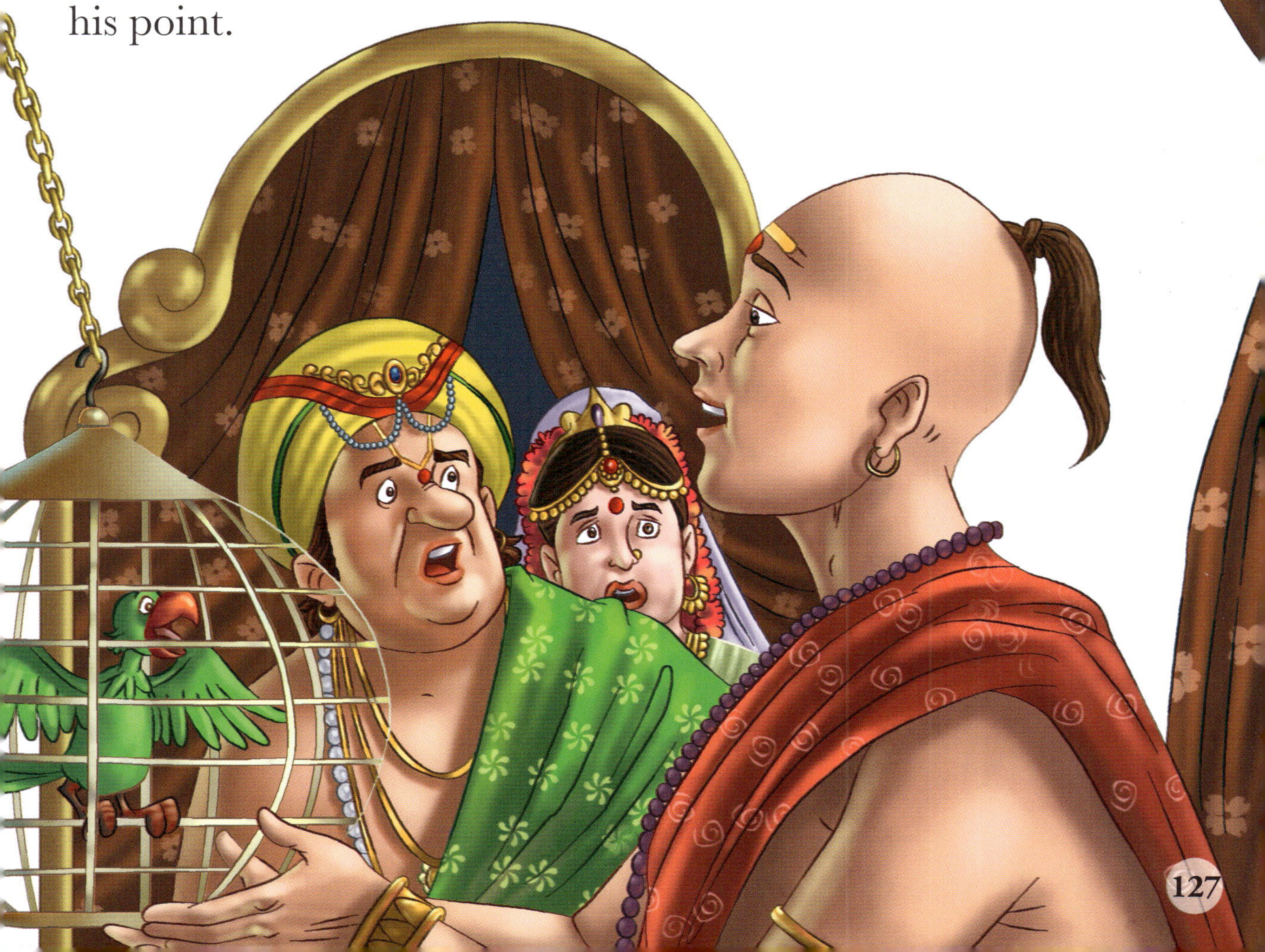

Tenali went in to another room and immediately came back with a cat. On seeing the cat, the parrot started making all sorts of sounds and began fluttering inside its cage. The queen was appalled and started asking the parrot to recite Hare Krishna. The parrot recited everything other than that!

The king then realised that Tenali was indeed speaking the truth. So he decided to let the parrot fly away into the sky. Tenali had proved his point once again.